the Calm before the... brainstorm

Stevie Ray

Punchline
Publications

Copyright © 2013 by Stephen M. Rentfrow
All rights reserved.
Printed in the United States of America.

No part of this book may be used or reproduced in any manner whatsoever without the written permission of the publisher except that portions may be used in broadcast or printed commentary or review when attributed fully to the author and publication by name.
For information address:

Punchline Publications
10700 Cambridge Ct.
Burnsville, MN 55337

Cover design by:
Arushti-The Design Studios, India

Punchline Publications is a division of
Stevie Ray's Improv Company
www.stevierays.org

Entertainment • Corporate Development • School of Improv
"Making it up as we go since 1989"

This book is dedicated to all the people who have ever had to sit in a room listening to someone ask, "Has anybody got any good ideas?"

Acknowledgements:

My wife, Kanitta, and step-daughter, Ondine. When it comes to brainstorming, I couldn't ask for better daily practice than keeping up with these two. I must also thank Kanitta for the many hours she spent proof-reading this book. Who would have thought I could miss so many commas?

My business partner and good friend, Pamela Mayne. Working together since 1989 to continually develop crazy ideas to keep our company growing is the best way to spend a career.

Gary Jader, who developed many of the concepts included in this book (but the best ideas are mine).

Contents

Preface

Read This First — 1

PART I
The Right Way to Play — 11

1 Preparing the Person — 17

2 Preparing the Group — 43

3 Preparing the Space — 93

PART II
The Eight Steps — 99

4 Laying the Foundation — 103
    Step One-Ultimate Goal
    Step Two-Immediate Objectives

5 Idea Generation — 113
    Step Three-Idea Generation
    Step Four-Incubation
    Step Five-Regeneration

6 Implementation 151
Step Six-Categorize
Step Seven-Prioritize & Strategize
Step Eight-Rewardize

Read This Last 163

Preface

A little about me.

Since no book can be completely free of the biases of the author, you should know a little about me so you can determine for yourself if what you are reading is fact or opinion. Hopefully this book will meld the two together into something useful for you.

In researching this book, I dug through various sources about neuroscience, psychology, management, and teamwork. I dislike books filled with those tiny footnote numbers at the end of sentences; it always feels like reading a college thesis where someone is trying to prove he read the assigned material. As such, I will spare you the numbers at the ends of sentences and simply let you know if there is a really cool book you should read.

As you read this book, you may notice that I lean towards favoring change over the status quo. I should balance that sentiment by stating that I have a healthy respect for tradition; in both business and in life. Frankly, if companies ran toward every new idea, most of those companies wouldn't last long. I do believe that small changes to even the most steadfast products can reap rewards. People around the world have been using trusty duct tape for decades. The original name was *duck tape* because the backing was made from cotton duck cloth. It was even helped use to build the Brooklyn Bridge in 1902. After so many years, who would think duct tape could be improved? Go to any craft store and now you'll find duct tape printed with cool designs, sports teams logos, and every color of the rainbow. Once people started using duct tape to create wallets, purses, and other crafts someone thought, "Hey! Let's make the old standard a little more modern." A small brainstorm resulted in a new and profitable avenue for sales.

I hate assumptions. As much as we need to rely on intuition—and sometimes blind faith—in order to make progress, when it comes to handing out advice I believe there is far too much acceptance of assumption as fact. I love it when children say, "Oh yeah. Who said so?" Followed with, "How does *he* know?" There is nothing in this book that hasn't been tested by either me or someone smarter than me. Enough for now, you'll learn more about me in the ensuing pages than is really necessary.

A little about Pamela Mayne.

In January of 1989, I received a call from a pair of colleagues who owned a comedy variety club. They wanted to move away from the day to day operations and remain owners. They wanted to know if I would take over as Managing Director. I asked who else would be running the club with me and they said that a woman named Pamela Mayne would be the Theatre/Box Office Manager. I had worked with Pamela on occasion and thought we would make a good team.

Shortly after taking over the club, we both realized that the business was in trouble. The finances were a mess and the company was going into debt. We expressed our concerns to the owners, who assured us that everything was under control and that we should continue the operations as instructed. By July of that year, they finally realized just how bad things were and wanted to get out of the business completely. The owners offered to sell the business to us for one dollar if we agreed to assume the debt and let them walk away. Not thinking clearly, we said yes and on August 18, 1989, we re-opened the club as *Stevie Ray's Improv Company*.

The foundation of the company was always improvisation. I had training in improvisation in college and also spent five years at *Dudley Riggs' Brave New Workshop (BNW)* in Minneapolis. The *Brave New Workshop* is to Minneapolis what *Second City* is to Chicago. I'll describe the Brave New Workshop more in detail later, but suffice it to say, it was the equivalent of a Bachelor's and Master's degree all rolled into one. My Ph.D. came from running my own company.

When Stevie Ray's opened, we saw improv training as a life skill, not just a performance art. We wanted our training and entertainment opportunities to benefit everyone, so we created four divisions: *Stevie Ray's Comedy Cabaret* for public performances, *The School of Improv* for classes, Corporate Entertainment, and Keynote Presentations & Customized Workshops.

A little about Gary.

One day in 2001, I was walking through a shopping mall and received a phone call. The caller introduced himself as Gary Jader and stated that he was an avid reader of my column (I write a monthly column in a nationwide business-oriented publication known as *The Business Journal* or *CityBusiness*, depending on the market). He said that he had researched my company on the internet and saw many similarities in our businesses; he wondered if there was "something we could do for each other." Having had my share of bogus sales calls, I told him to send me an e-mail about what he had in mind and I politely hung up. I thought that would get rid of him.

Luckily for me, Gary is a persistent fellow. Thirty seconds later, my phone rang again. It was Gary. He promised me that he wasn't trying to sell me something, he just had a very strong feeling that our business interests were similar enough that we could be of use to each other. I agreed to meet him for lunch. By the end of the two hours, we agreed that he would start taking our improv classes. Not long afterwards, he joined our board of directors and started participating in the corporate training division of our company. Gary worked with us to expand our existing list of corporate training offerings and we co-presented workshops together for a few years. Other opportunities lead Gary in a different direction, but *Stevie Ray's Improv Company* still counts Gary as one of our most valuable veterans, and I still claim many of his great ideas as my own.

A little about Kanitta and Ondine.

This has nothing to do with brainstorming, but it's a great story. I met Kanitta during a corporate retreat at a resort in northern Minnesota. The company she worked for hired me to conduct a workshop in the afternoon and provide entertainment in the evening. Kanitta was one of the regional managers organizing the retreat. I noticed this dark-haired beauty as soon as she entered the conference room. Typically, corporate speakers do not get to know the attendees at a company event, but this company also hired our comedy troupe to perform that evening. With nothing to do all afternoon, I thought I would sit around bored until the troupe arrived that night.

After my afternoon workshop, I turned around and there was Kanitta, inviting me to join her and the rest of the staff for a company pontoon boat ride. Surprise, surprise, there was an open seat right next to Kanitta. We struck up a friendship, with a spark, but she lived in Chicago and I lived in Minneapolis and neither one was moving. She went her way and I went mine. Twelve years later, I was thinking about all the changes that life brings and I kept thinking about *the one that got away*. I sent a letter (yes, hand written on paper and everything) to the last address I had for her.

Two days later, I received a phone call. Kanitta said that very week her best friend asked her who she would most love to hear from again and my name popped up. Taking all this as a sign, she moved to Minneapolis and we got married at the same resort where we first met. Her daughter, Ondine, was only five years old at the time, but quickly took to riding on my shoulders and waking me up in the morning by pounding me with a pillow.

Brainstorming in my house involves trying to win debates with two very stubborn females. Ondine is also a budding artist so when it comes to playtime, she invariably wants us all to do projects such as inventing a new arcade game out of construction paper and glue. I stand corrected; those two have a great deal to do with brainstorming in my life.

Read This First

I can describe the typical approach to brainstorming and innovation by quoting what one CEO said to me. His company had hired Gay Jader and I to conduct a workshop with his staff and he quietly pulled us aside and said, "We want a lot of new and exciting ideas, but we don't really want to change anything." It reminds me of the old saying, "Everybody wants to get to Heaven, but nobody wants to die." When it comes to brainstorming, in order to experience the Heaven of fantastic new ideas, something has to die; usually the old, tried-and-true ways of doing things.

> *At about the age of nine I decided never to believe anything because it was convenient.*
> Keith Johnstone
> Author of *Impro*
> (More about him later)

Kodak, Lucent Technologies, and Xerox are all sad examples of what happens when companies refuse to give up safety in order to venture down a new path. All three organizations were at the top of their industries, but refused to institute new ideas or technologies. None are but shadows of their former selves. In the 1980's, the east coast technology firm DEC was second only to IBM in size and scope. After the president of DEC announced with certainty that "personal computers will never be popular," things started going south. Compaq eventually purchased what was left of DEC.

The myth about brainstorming is, when needs arise, we respond with solutions. The more drastic the need, the more ideas will magically appear. People often believe that the importance of the outcome will help the group focus. Urgency will ensure that we invent our way out of trouble. However, the fact is even when a solution to a problem is presented, we resist. For example, during the horse-and-buggy era, pollution from horses was a terrible problem in metropolitan areas. Urine on the streets caused a stifling stench and there were literally mountains of dung on the outskirts of cities. When the automobile was first introduced, it was not only reviled because it was an unfamiliar technology, but there was a nationwide scare that all those involved in the horse industry would be left without work. Listen to current debates about possible replacements for the odor-causing, environment-harming car, and you hear the same concerns about job loss and new technology. Sadly, necessity is not the mother of invention.

Dr. Stuart Brown is a medical doctor, psychologist, clinical researcher, and the founder of the National Institute for Play. For years, he has studied play behavior and its effect on the brain; conducting research on thousands of individuals from all walks of life. Dr. Brown discovered that necessity doesn't spark creativity. In his book, *Play*, he states, "Necessity isn't the mother of invention, it's more like the first date."

The CEO I previously referred to above (who said he wanted new ideas, but didn't want to change anything) ran a large printing company. We'll call him Chuck ('cause that's his name). Chuck said, "If we don't do something soon, the competition will bury us. The trouble is, I can't get any good ideas out of my executive team. Can you help us?" Gary and I could sense by his demeanor who the real problem was—you probably guessed it yourself—so we were eager to help this company brainstorm the right way.

As we sat and watched, Chuck gathered twelve of his top executives and started with, "Okay everyone, we're in trouble. If we don't do something big—and fast—those guys at Company X will run right over us. So, who's got a good idea?" The group sat stunned while Chuck hovered over a dry-erase board with marker in hand, ready to jot down the next million dollar idea.

Fred was the first to step up to the firing line with, "Well, we could branch out into Shelbyville. They are a completely under-served market." Immediately, Chuck pounced with, "That idea is okay, but we don't really have the budget for expansion right now. But keep the ideas coming!" Eugene offered, "How about we put some effort into those new re-usable body stickers I see the kids wearing? They seem to be popular." "That's all right," said Chuck. "We just don't have the means for new R&D. But keep 'em coming!"

This went on for about thirty minutes, with the executive team tossing up targets so Chuck could blast them with his scatter-gun (*shotgun* to you young-uns). After the meeting adjourned, he pulled us aside and said, "You see? I can't get any good ideas out of my team. What do you think is wrong?" It is hard when the person responsible for the problem is asking what the problem is. We promised to help Chuck with a new method if he promised to keep an open mind. I'll tell you how it turned out later, but first let's talk about brainstorming itself.

Brainstorming didn't just happen all by its lonesome. The process most people use was introduced by an advertising executive, Alex F. Osborn. In 1953 he published *Applied Imagination* in which he detailed his approach to creativity and brainstorming, along with a set of rules. All of Osborne's rules were meant to deliver what he considered to be the ultimate goal of all brainstorming; a high volume of ideas. He believed that quantity begot quality. It seemed logical that the more ideas you had to choose from, the greater the chance for something innovative to appear. You just had to dig through the mud to find the jewel.

To make brainstorm sessions more productive, Osborn also demanded the *suspension of judgment*. He believed, as do many today, that any critique would kill an idea and stifle the creativity of the group. He also called for specificity. A brainstorm session should focus on one issue at a time so as not to dilute the process.

This all sounds quite logical. The wonderful thing about most people is, if we hear something that sounds logical we tend to believe it without need of further proof. However, many aspects of Osborn's approach to brainstorming are flawed. As early as 1958, studies at Yale showed that subjects working alone developed almost twice as many ideas as those from group brainstorming sessions; and the ideas developed by solo workers were judged to be more effective and creative than those from the group. This doesn't mean that the brainstorm model is tragically flawed; it simply means that it needs some tweaking in order to help people produce cool new ideas.

Knowing how the brain works is a good start. As I mentioned before, many modern-day "facts" are actually unchallenged assumptions. It is amazing that someone—anyone—can state an opinion and, if it is repeated often enough, the opinion becomes "fact." Psychology and neuroscience are not immune to this trend. Advances in medical technology have debunked many long held myths about the brain. One myth was that the brain is a static organism, wired at birth and set for life. Now we know the brain is a fluid organism, able to re-wire and adapt throughout one's entire lifetime.

That's the good news. The bad news is that while the brain can learn new things, it can easily become stuck in old patterns of thinking. Humans have evolved very quickly on a social basis, but very slowly biologically. Most of our brain's processes are still set at the Hunter-Gatherer stage of human evolution. Scientists describe humans' time on Earth by this metaphor. If the Earth's entire timetable were compared to a single calendar year, human life would occupy the final second on the clock on December 31st. (Kind of takes the ego down a peg, doesn't it?)

Because our brain is still set at the Hunter-Gatherer stage, its prime concern is stuck at that era. The brain's prime concern is safety/security. For most of our evolution, safety/security was the most difficult state to achieve, yet the most important. It has been discovered that the brain values safety/security even above freedom. Remember when you and some friends had the freedom to decide where to have lunch? After thirty minutes of debate, someone always says, "Somebody just decide!" When push comes to shove, we prefer safety/security. Throughout the day, the brain spends most of its energy on the look-out for threats, real or perceived.

The brain's love of safety/security would have an obvious negative effect on brainstorming. Why would an organism so concerned with safety/security want to develop ideas that risk entering the unknown? Safety/Security is all about staying with what you know; using what works. This is why people shunned the automobile as a replacement for the horse-and-buggy. *Better the devil you know than the devil you don't.*

Here is another tidbit about the brain that helps to understand why new ideas can be frustrating; even scary. The brain's least efficient function is information processing. Processing data is a high-level task for the brain. It certainly is capable of engaging in the brainy stuff (how else would we have 3D video games?), but the brain prefers simpler functions. As such, the brain's most efficient function is pattern recognition. The brain loves to discern patterns in the environment and follow them. Patterned behavior leads to productivity, lower stress, and a simpler life. We have all experienced brain shut-down while sitting in a meeting that was filled with data and statistics. Not long into the meeting you started praying that all the information would be in a hand-out. Too much information and the brain shouts "Enough!"

How does patterned thinking affect creativity? Obviously, being innovative requires breaking patterns instead of following them, but patterned thinking leads to another outcome that hinders brainstorming. Because the brain hates information and loves patterns, it is easier for the brain to *remember* than it is to *imagine*. Imagining something new requires a lot of processing, memory is simply a neural pathway in the brain, a pattern of electrical impulses. The brain's love of pattern leads to the oft-heard, "Why can't we just do it the way we've always done it?"

It isn't that certain people are stuck doing things the old way, all humans are. The good thing is, it is not too difficult to break away from the brain's patterned way of thinking. The key is to manage the stress of the brainstorming process. Some people try to eliminate stress from brainstorming all-together, believing that it kills creativity. These people try to make the entire process fun and silly. Fun certainly does lead to creativity, but an atmosphere of only fun lacks focus. The fact is a small amount of stress is actually good for people. In the right amounts, stress helps us focus; it enhances creativity. Stress even enhances fun. Most of the games we play contain a moderate amount of stress; the anxiety of winning vs. losing, not knowing what the outcome of the game might be; time limits, buzzers, twists, and surprises. These tricks create good levels of stress. Elevated stress, however, has the opposite effect. Too much stress and you can't think, create, or communicate ideas. It is up to the facilitator to manage the stress in the room; we'll cover that more in detail later.

The first step to a more productive brainstorm session is to understand that the brain needs a certain environment in order to produce creative ideas. It is also important to understand that creative ideas are not the product of "Ah ha" moments. The image of a scientist messing around in the lab until he or she stumbles upon the cure of the millennia is not just a myth, it is damaging to those who need new ideas for their organization.

Most innovative ideas are the product of months or years of refining, retooling, and hard work. Creativity and innovation are not instant. The group or the facilitator who expects it upon demand is not only unrealistic, but setting up the group for failure. The classic 1950's model of brainstorming proved unrealistic soon after its inception because people expected it to produce great results all by itself. The real work starts after the meeting is over and can take some time to bear fruit.

The following is a step-by-step method for facilitating productive brainstorming. While preparing the book, I considered changing the term brainstorming into something new (lately, many people use the term *ideation*). For ease of understanding I will use the word *brainstorming*. Just remember, the process described in this book might be different than the brainstorming with which you are familiar.

PART I

The Right Way to Play

> *Play is the stick that stirs the drink.*
> Dr. Stuart Brown
> Author of *Play*

An atmosphere of play is crucial to creativity. While researching his book *Play*, Dr. Stuart Brown delved into the effects of play on the brain. To establish a foundation of understanding about the subject, he liked to ask people, "What is the opposite of play?" Invariably the answer was, "Work." However, his research discovered that—in terms of neuroscience and psychology—work and play are not each other's opposites. They are two pillars that combine to support a healthy brain.

At first, work and play seem opposite. Work is outcome-based, whereas play has no outcome. Work is timed and structured; play in lightly organized, but can be easily changed. Rather than being time sensitive, play frees us from thinking about time. Work is done for a stated purpose; play is done for its own sake. Beyond that, the opposites end.

Work provides us with focus, a feeling of accomplishment and satisfaction (unless you work for the Department of Motor Vehicles). Play releases healthy chemicals in the brain that allow it to function. If a person goes for long periods of time without engaging in play behavior, those healthy chemicals cease, and the brain begins to decline. As Dr. Brown puts it, the opposite of play is not work; the opposite of play is depression. If you want productive brainstorming, you must strike a balance between focused, outcome-based activity and non-outcome, play behavior.

During brainstorming, playing a seemingly purposeless activity can cause the mind to create surprise connections, and develop new solutions to problems. Traditional brainstorming often forces so much focus on the problem that the group becomes frozen. Play is a way to break that log jam.

A wonderful story is told by Dr. Brown that illustrates just how important play behavior is to the health of any mammal. Some years ago, a sled-dog owner, a musher, in northern Canada was afraid for the safety of his dogs. That winter was difficult for polar bears because the sea had not yet frozen so they couldn't get to food supplies. Without a frozen ice cap, bears are unable to walk the great distance needed to find seals and other prey. If a stray bear happened into the village, sled dogs would make a great meal.

One day, the musher noticed a polar bear wandering into camp, but it wasn't making the usual bee-line drive for food. The polar bear's gait was circular and its demeanor non-threatening. Upon seeing the bear, one of the sled dogs hunched down and wagged its tail to signal an invitation to play; most likely responding to the playful gait of the bear. What happened next was astonishing. The starving polar bear rolled around in the snow, romping with the dogs.

Rather than bite each other aggressively, both mammals nipped lightly as four-legged animals will do while playing. At one point, the bear even laid on his back to signal he needed a rest from the activity. After a while, the bear grew tired and loped away. This scene was repeated every day for a week until the ice formed and the bear could go hunt for food. How strong is the need for play that a starving animal will forego food in order to satisfy this basic need? For all of us, play is just as nourishing as food.

So why would anyone need instruction on play? Don't you just *do* it? The answer is yes—if you are a child. Most adults need a big push in that direction. Adults place such a premium on outcome that playtime must wait until we have everything checked off the to-do list. However, given that the very act of play can prepare a person to meet the demands of a constantly changing environment, play itself should be on the to-do list.

Jonah Lehrer is an Oxford University Rhodes Scholar, neuroscience researcher, and author of *Imagine: How Creativity Works*. In *Imagine*, Lehrer talks about how play involves letting go. Letting go of the focus on immediate outcomes deactivates the dorsolateral prefrontal cortex. This part of the brain controls the constraint system; deactivating this "handcuff on the brain" enables improvisation. When you turn off this brain censor, ideas start to flow. Children brainstorm better because their right prefrontal cortex has not yet been activated. This cortex of the brain usually fires up around age ten. Teachers often report a *Fourth Grade Slump*: the brain's censor has kicked in and creativity takes a back seat to making sure the answers are correct on the test.

Prior to this slump, kids are more concerned about process than outcome. As long as everyone is having fun, things are great. When my step-daughter, Ondine, was nine years old, my wife, Kanitta, took her to a park to play. Another nine-year old girl was already there (good thing too, because boys are stinky). Ondine ran up to the other girl and said, "Hi. Want to be friends?" In no time, they were playing. Now Ondine has a new BFF. (If you don't know what BFF stands for, you are ancient!) Compare that to the last time you walked into the cafeteria at work. I call it the *High School Cafeteria Walk*. Just like in high school, you grab your tray and start scanning the room for anyone you might know. You walk past empty chairs at any number of tables, ignoring people because they work in other departments or are dressed strangely. Finally you spot spotting one person you know; your lifeboat in a sea of strangers. This behavior is not entirely unreasonable. A Hunter-Gatherer reaction of suspicion toward strangers is to be expected; how else would we protect our family and our stuff? It does, however, hinder working as a group.

In *Imagine*, Lehrer explains that we are most creative when alpha waves are being generated in the brain. These magic waves inspire creativity and innovation. Alpha waves are at their peak when we are engaged in a relaxing, no-thought activity like walking or taking a warm shower. In fact, most people have their best ideas while showering (unless you're in the Navy, then you are worried that your commanding officer is going to shut off your water). The reason play generates such great ideas is because it is an activity that doesn't matter. The act of play helps to generate alpha waves that send the brain into creative hyper-drive (that last sentence was for *Star Trek* fans).

Back to the point that innovation is more of a process than an "Ah ha" discovery; play behavior creates those weird connections that, when examined, create useful ideas. As Isaac Asimov says, "The most exciting phrase in science is not 'Eureka,' but 'That's funny.'" So what exactly is the right way to play? Quite simply, ignore the outcome. Too often we get bogged down with the question of, "Where are we going with this?" To be sure, a useful product, service, or system is the ultimate goal of brainstorming, but concentrating on the outcome at the wrong part of the process will kill creativity. You never hear children say, "We can't play Tag yet. We don't even have a mission statement!"

An atmosphere of productive play is one where, at precisely the moments needed, the group disengages from the goal and does some good old time wasting. I'll talk about when those moments occur when we get into the Eight Steps. First, let's lay more groundwork by making sure the three elements of brainstorming are well prepared; the Person, the Group, and the Space.

CHAPTER 1

Preparing the Person

Humans are mammals. Mammals, being social creatures, take their cue on how to behave from those around them. Humans are considered *ultra-social mammals* because we live in larger groups than any other mammal on the planet. As such, we are finely tuned to the reactions of those around us. Most of the decisions we make about how to behave are based on how we think our behavior will be viewed by our social group. This makes it easy to fit in and get along, but can be a hindrance when it comes to suggesting a wacky new idea that just popped into our head. For productive brainstorming, each individual must be in a mental state that will encourage creativity and eager participation from every participant.

What state do you live in?

Mammals generally go through their days in one of two states of being: a state of nervousness or a state of comfort. Which state you are in will determine your ability to do almost any task. A state of comfort leads to creativity, trust, love, and overall well-being. Extreme comfort is not good.

Extreme comfort leads to complacency. Humans need a little excitement—a small amount of tension—in order to be productive and find joy in life.

If, however, minor tension is allowed to build into nervousness or stress, we shut down. Too much tension leads to distrust, dislike, and the fight-or-flight response of "Get me out of here!" Brainstorming always carries a measure of tension; a little bit of "What's going to happen next?" No one can be absolutely sure if the brainstorming is going to work. They are curious about what strange ideas might come out. This kind of tension is healthy, and a good facilitator's job is to monitor the group to make sure that excited tension doesn't cross over into nervousness or stress.

Here is another tidbit about the brain that will help to understand instant reactions to ideas. The part of the brain that handles fear and anger is the amygdala. The amygdala is a base part of the brain's system, meaning it reacts without thought. The amygdala has been responsible for keeping humans alive on this planet since we first came down from the trees five or ten years ago. If you are walking in the woods and come upon a snake, your amygdala senses the snake and signals to your legs to run long before your cerebral cortex creates the connection: *Snake equals danger. Appropriate response; get the heck out of here.*

When working together, people either play and have fun or they don't have fun, which creates stress. Stress activates the amygdala. When the amygdala signals danger, creativity is lost. If you are being chased by a wild boar (and who hasn't been?), you don't want your cerebral cortex wasting time by thinking of the most creative solution to the problem, you just want your amygdala to say, "Legs, run!" Keeping brainstorming fun is not just to provide a happy environment for everyone, it is vital to creating a productive session.

In general, the female amygdala response is twice as strong as a male's. The female amygdala response also typically lasts twice as long as the male's. The theory is that females have historically been responsible for caring for the family while men have been the hunters. A strong danger response is good when watching over a bunch of children, since the primary goal is to keep the brood away from harm. An overwhelming amygdala response is not good when you are hunting. Panic when hunting prevents a successful kill, which isn't good when your family is waiting around the microwave.

If a fear/danger response starts building within the individual, there are two ways to handle it; distraction or incubation. You can distract away from the danger-causing stimuli by playing a game. Laughter immediately dissipates the amygdala response. This is why it is never a good idea for a facilitator who senses tension in the room to say,

"Come on, let's focus on this problem." This does not dissipate the amygdala response, it only heightens it. This rule does not mean you can't have lively debate. In fact, debate is a good thing (we'll discuss that in more detail later). You must make sure the debate stays centered on the issue and does not lead to attacks on the individual.

Incubation involves getting away from the group and allowing the brain to work through the danger response and return to calm. Incubation is used to diminish the damaging effects of an alarmed brain. It follows the same tactic parents use when separating children who are the midst of a fight. Time-outs are very helpful for the amygdala; which method you choose—distraction or incubation—depends on the person and the situation.

I'm in a Whole-Brain state of mind

As we age, our brains change function. Youthful brains are meant to absorb information quickly, but they can't organize the information very well. The more we age, the more efficient our brains become. Like a beginning tennis player will expend too much energy for a simple stroke, a youthful brain will work extra hard soaking up everything it experiences; not knowing what to do with the information. An experienced tennis player uses only those muscles needed for a perfect backhand, remaining relaxed and smooth. An older brain also decides which centers or cortexes are needed for the task at hand and leaves the rest relaxed and dormant. If you are a "numbers person" who doesn't deal in words very often, your thalamus might stay alert while the left temporal lobe sleeps.

This scenario is a bit of a generalization, but specialized skills can tend to put the brain on a singular path. This is great for efficiency, but tends to leave older brains unable to think outside of their area of expertise. The good thing is that brains are wonderfully malleable and adaptive. It doesn't take much to shake loose the cobwebs and get your brain inventing new tracks of thinking. You just have to coax your noggin in the right direction.

The best way to combat *segmented thinking* (using only a few centers of the brain at a time), is to engage in *whole-brain activity*. Whole-brain activity is when every center of the brain fires at the same time. The brain doesn't engage in whole-brain activity very often because it is an inefficient use of energy. The brain is very good at conserving energy, especially since twenty percent of the body's entire energy output is used by the brain. The way to engage whole-brain activity is to play a game that contains two qualities.

The first quality is that the game must contain randomness and unpredictability. Any time the brain is met with a surprise, it must wake up all the cortexes in order to meet the challenge. This happens every time we hit a detour on our favorite route to work. Our regular route is the best, not necessarily because it is the shortest, but because it requires no thinking. We can set our brain on auto-pilot and think about more important things during the drive. When our expected pattern of driving is thrown off, we must now improvise a new route to work. Randomness provides a healthy wake-up for the mind, but it frustrates adults. We usually plan our day so there are no surprises. Getting accustomed to occasional chaos is healthy for the brain and helpful for brainstorming.

The second quality of a whole-brain game is that there must be no outcome of the activity; no stated purpose. If you play the game Monopoly, you know what the outcome is right from the start; try to make your partners go bankrupt. There is a process and order to the game, plus an outcome. An outcome or purpose for an activity causes the brain to segment the experience in the proper area. This helps with cognitive learning, but inhibits whole-brain activity. A stated outcome is helpful for cognitive growth—learning a new skill, mastering a second language, playing crossword puzzles—but cognitive growth is different than whole-brain activity. Combining cognitive learning and whole-brain activity will help you keep a healthy brain in your skull for a long time.

Children play whole-brain games by choice. The game of Tag is random, unpredictable, and has no outcome. There really is no winner in Tag, you just keep playing until bedtime. Adults prefer process, order, and outcome; so we play card games or board games with definite structure and winners and losers. Whole-brain games are similar to music. A musician learns scales in order to build a foundation of skills, and then applies those skills to play music. A good musician, however, will return to practicing scales to keep basic skills sharp. Whole-brain games are scales for the brain. The fun part is, whereas cognitive learning is often difficult and tiring, whole-brain activity is subconscious. All the benefits happen without you having to work at it; you simply play a game. If you want a book of games, my book *Quick Thinking for Any Situation* has a bunch. You can also look online for "improv warm-up games." Improvisational exercises are whole-brain in nature. Just remember, don't expect to *feel* during a whole-brain game. Since the benefits are subconscious, people often finish the game and say, "What happened? It didn't feel like we did anything." The only thing you will likely feel after a whole-brain game is exhilarated—you will laugh and be energized.

Make it up as you go

In order to create cool new ideas, a person must be in an improvisational state of mind. My company, *Stevie Ray's Improv Company*, has been in the business of improvisation since 1989. Improvisation is a term used by jazz musicians when they go "off the chart" and create music spontaneously. It is also a style of comedy (most commonly seen on the T.V. show *Whose Line is it Anyway?*). Improvisation actually dates back centuries. Theatre professionals are often referred to as *thespians* out of respect for Thespis, the man who is considered the first actor. Ancient Greek theatre was much different than the scripted plays of today. Instead of characters acting individual parts, a group known as the *Chorus* would speak in unison, describing the actions of the plot (usually accounts of great battles or stories from mythology). During one performance, Thespis took a chance and stepped away from the chorus and spoke lines. No one knows exactly what he said, but he played one of the characters of the plot. Since there was no script for him to follow, Thespis created his lines on the spot; not only was he the first actor, he was the first improviser.

Improvisation became more structured in 16th century Italy with the theatre style of *Commedia dell'Arte*. Comedy troupes would tour Italy and, instead of performing scripted plays, they would improvise comedies based on general plots called *scenarios*. A scenario could be as simple as:

- Husband goes out to the field to work the farm.
- Wife has secret lover arrive at the house.
- Husband comes home early.
- Lover must hide in as many places as possible as
- Husband moves around the house.
- Husband discovers Lover.
- Wife creates fake identity for Lover as a ruse.
- Lover escapes and everyone is happy.

Improvisation today generally consists of a group of performers creating instant comedy scenes, called "sketches", based on ideas called out from the audience. Many people confuse improv with stand-up comedy, which is different in that stand-up involves a solo performer delivering prepared material.

Modern improvisation had a number of founders. Viola Spolin was a theatre teacher and educator in Chicago in the late 1930s. In her work with youths at various community centers, she developed games in order to help them develop mental and social skills. These games were later turned into theatrical exercises which she published in *Improvisation for the Theatre*. Her son, Paul Sills, used these techniques when he opened the *Second City* theatre in Chicago in 1959 with Roger Bowen, Eugene Troobnik, Dave Shepherd, and Bernie Sahlins.

Dudley Riggs in Minneapolis is another major figure in improvisation, but where Spolin's work was spawned from working with youth, Dudley's improvisational techniques were borne from the theatre stage. Dudley's family was circus performers. He grew up on the high wire and the trapeze, touring from town to town across the country. In the winters when the circus would shut down for the season, Dudley toured the country as part of a vaudeville comedy troupe. Performing comedy in a vaudeville house was not easy; audiences loved to heckle. Dudley's comedy troupe was always trying to figure out how to better handle the hecklers. One day Dudley had a moment of inspiration; instead of trying to shut the hecklers down, why not use them? He suggested to his troupe that they ask the audience to shout things (since they were going to shout anyway) and use the heckling as comedy material. His troupe thought he was crazy. Nevertheless, at the next show, the troupe brought a large trunk onstage filled with hats, jackets, and other odd costumes. Dudley began with, "Good afternoon ladies and gentlemen, it is great to be here in (insert name of town). Tell me, who do you hate here the most?" The audience shouted out, "The mayor!" Riggs replied, "Very well. We give you 'A Day at the Mayor's Office.'"

The troupe pulled out costumes and props from the trunk and began to spoof the mayor, to the delight of the audience. So was borne *Dudley Riggs' Instant Theatre Company*. His new style of comedy was an immediate hit and Dudley and his troupe toured the country every winter. One winter, Dudley's agent had bad news. The agent hadn't been able to book any dates for the troupe. His group was stuck in New York City without a winter tour. Not wanting to sit idle, Dudley rented an empty store front so the troupe could rehearse and stay sharp. Before long, passersby were peeking in the window to watch the antics; some even offered to pay to watch. This piqued the imagination of the entrepreneurial Riggs. He did some dealing and got his troupe booked for a run at a local night club.

The show was a hit. Later, when Dudley was considering where to build a permanent theatre, he remembered that he always loved Minneapolis. So in 1958 he opened *Dudley Riggs' Café Espresso* in Minneapolis where he sold coffee from the first espresso machine ever to operate in Minnesota. Dudley featured satirical comedy in order to keep coffee-buying guests in the café longer. Later, he opened *Dudley Riggs' Brave New Workshop* which remains a stalwart in the Minneapolis theatre scene to this day. Dudley often says that he ran away from the circus to join a family.

Beyond its application as a performance art, improvisation helps people think more creatively, work better in teams, and speak with confidence. Most schools of improvisation follow a classic rule that is also a key to brainstorming; the rule of *"Yes, and..."* When students learn the basics of improvisation, they are encouraged to avoid *negating*, or shutting down ideas from their partners. They instead work on accepting an idea (the *"yes"* part), then adding to the idea (the *"and"* part). By everyone accepting and building, a single idea can grow to unexpected and delightful results.

The hard part is that saying yes to someone else's idea isn't easy. With some people's ideas, it is downright torturous. Because our brains have a built-in mechanism for creating patterns, we always think we know the direction things should go. And, if someone goes in the *wrong* direction, we feel the need to correct them; not follow them down the path to obvious destruction. In the world of improvisation, the tendency to plan ahead and try to direct the outcome is called *playwriting*. Only a playwright knows every word that will be spoken; he or she wrote the script. Playwriting makes sure there are no mistakes, but it kills creativity. Improv prefers a more creative *"yes, and..."* environment. Quite simply, traditional theatre *interprets*, improvisation *creates*. Please note that I will use the terms *improv* and *improvisation* interchangeably.

At *Stevie Ray's Improv Company*, we built *"yes, and..."* into our business model. My business partner and I follow a one word business plan, the word "Okay." If someone offers a business suggestion, we say "okay" and give the idea a try. This philosophy has led to some of the greatest successes of our company and some of the most interesting lessons (we substitute *failure* with *lesson learned*. It's a more productive way of thinking).

Our entire foray into corporate training was the result of saying okay. Our *School of Improv* was designed for working professionals. We always thought of improv as a skill for the real world, not just for the stage, so we marketed our classes mainly to non-performers. One exercise we teach in beginning classes is called *Simultaneous Dialogue*. It is a difficult split-focus exercise that helps sharpen listening and reaction skills. One student came to class and said, "You know that split-focus game we played last week? I used it at work. I was talking to a client on the phone and overheard another conversation in the office. What I overheard had serious implications for my client. I was able to stay focused and still fold the new information into the conversation. It ended up saving my client a lot of money."

After he finished recounting the event he asked, "Have you guys ever thought of expanding beyond classes? Instead of just getting individuals to come to your school, you should approach companies and offer group workshops for staff members." Staying true to our business plan, we said, "Okay." We didn't know how to do it, but we knew the idea was worth a try. Within a year, the new Corporate Services division became the fastest growing and most profitable part of our company. We have taught workshops to over a thousand companies in eight countries; all because we used the rule of *"yes, and..."* and said okay to one man's idea. That's why we have kept the same company slogan since we opened, *Making it up as we go since 1989.*

When you watch an improv performance, the speed and mental agility of the performers can make it look very difficult. To be sure, performing improv at a professional level takes quite of bit of training, but we are all born to make things up as we go. When children are allowed to play without adult intervention, they usually improvise a game. "You go over there and do this while I stand here and do that." They cooperate and blend ideas together until the game takes shape. They make up new rules as needed or get rid of rules that take the fun out of the game. The older we get, the more we rely on structure and rules. We don't lose the ability to make things up or improvise, but we need more coaxing to let go of our security blankets of process and organization.

The thing that surprises most people when they first learn improvisation is how much structure is involved. People expect the process to be entirely free flowing, like hippies dancing around a bonfire. They are shocked to discover there are rules in improvisation. They soon discover what all creative professionals know, that rules do not inhibit creativity, they enhance it.

In his later years, before passing away in 2008 at the age of 81, Paul Sills (the founder of *Second City*) taught special workshops in improvisation at his farm house in northern Wisconsin. He would accept only sixteen applicants at a time ,from around the country, for a one-week intensive improv retreat. I was lucky enough to be accepted one year. So I arrived at his farmhouse to meet sixteen strangers from across the US and Canada. Sills had actually converted a barn on his farmstead into a theatre; making the classic theatre line. "My dad's got a barn and my mom can sew costumes. Let's start a theatre" a reality. Sills started off the training by telling us, "Creativity is borne of structure." He explained that true creativity comes from providing a framework upon which to build ideas. Too much empty space leaves people lost. Having guidelines gives us just enough security to experiment.

At *Stevie Ray's Improv Company*, we follow the classic Eight Rules of Improv that I first learned from Dudley Riggs. Note: If you speak to an improv professional about rules of improvisation, you may spark a debate. Companies range from Three Rules to Ten Rules to "We don't need no sticking rules!" Don't get caught up in the debate, just smile, nod, and back away slowly. Every improv company follows at least a few guidelines to provide a foundation upon which to create. The eight rules below come from a combination of the early years of *Second City*—actually from its predecessor *The Compass*—and Dudley Riggs' Theatres.

The Eight Rules of Improv

1) Trust

First, trust yourself.

Next, trust your partner or you will inhibit his or her participation or try to control the outcome.

2) Don't Negate or Deny

A Negation is opposing a truth that someone else establishes.

    Performer 1: "Hi Dad. I'm home."

    Performer 2: "I'm not your dad."

A Denial is opposing an idea with, "No" or "That won't work."

3) Don't Ask Questions
Asking questions places the burden on others to create; you should instead make a strong statement.

4) Stay Actional
A sedate body slows down the brain. When in doubt, go to your space and use an object. Move and creativity will follow.

5) Make Assumptions
Rather than wait for permission from others, assume you know all you need to know; be the one to get things started.

6) Give & Take
Share the stage. Don't do all the talking or all the listening. Be prepared to play whatever part is needed to keep things moving.

7) Focus (Listen, Watch, Concentrate)
Be fully part of the process. Be as attentive to others as you expect them to be attentive to you.

8) Work to the Top of Your Intelligence
In performance this rules prohibits cheap humor for shock value. For training it reminds us that we must do our homework. We must continue to learn, to keep up on local and world events. Creativity requires knowledge.

Only in the narrowest of interpretations do the rules of improvisation apply solely to the performance of *improv*. Obviously, negating is harmful to a scene. If one person begins the scene by calling the other person "Dad" and the partner responds with, "I'm not your dad," that negation kills the scene. It is clear that the partner who responded with "I'm not your dad" had a specific idea for the scene, but didn't speak first. Rather than accepting his partner's line, he stopped the scene in its tracks in an attempt to force his idea. One of the most difficult lessons in improvisational training is to let go of your original idea to accept whatever is spoken first.

In real life however, negating comes in the form of the phrase "Yeah, but..." "Yes, and..." allows different ideas to combine. "Yeah, but..." destroys ideas. Getting rid of "yeah, but..." is one of the toughest challenges in improv training. It is also one of the toughest phrases to remove from everyday use. Replace "yeah, but..." with "yes, and..." in your daily language and you will force your brain to think at a higher level. You will see much better outcomes in meetings and regular conversations.

Trust is at the top of the list of rules because it is the most important—and the most tenuous—condition to establish among a group. It can take months to develop trust in a group, but it only takes minutes to destroy it. The first step is to trust yourself. If you don't fully trust your ideas, you will present them weakly. Any idea presented with trepidation signals to the group that the idea is not worth listening to. This not only weakens the idea presented, but weakens the entire group's ability to participate with confidence.

Remember the discussion about mammals taking our cue for behavior from the rest of the pack? That holds true for presenting ideas. As much as we like to think that we respond only based on the worth of the idea, we don't. We do not weigh pros and cons and make a rational, informed decision. More often, we respond to the manner in which the idea is presented.

Robert Cialdini is a Regents' Professor of Psychology at Arizona State University where he also earned the distinction of Graduate Distinguished Research Professor. In his book, *Influence: Science and Practice*, Cialdini discusses just what causes us to accept some ideas and reject others. Rather than using our advanced intellect to weigh pros and cons (too much work), our brains respond to triggers that engage an automatic response. Cialdini explains that we have *fixed-action patterns* in our brains that dictate our behavior. These reactions are like pre-recorded tapes waiting for the right trigger to activate them. Dr. Cialdini calls it the *Click, Whirr* response. A stimulus triggers us, *click;* then the taped response plays, *whirr.*

Jonathan Haidt is an Associate Professor of Psychology at the University of Virginia and co-editor of *Flourishing: Positive Psychology and the Life Well-Lived*. In his book,

The Happiness Hypothesis, Haidt describes this process as the brain's *Like-o-Meter*, (also called the *Approach/Withdraw Response*). We are wired to process sensory input and instantly decide whether we like or dislike it. This process in the brain was developed to keep us safe by instantly disliking and withdrawing from dangerous situations. This accounts for the weird feeling you get in your gut when you meet a prospective mate whom you don't feel quite right about. When the *thinking* part of your brain says, "Well, I guess there is nothing really wrong with this person," you date them anyway. Six months later—as you are extricating yourself from the new wacko in your life—you ask yourself why you didn't trust your gut. In most cases, your gut thinks more clearly than your cerebral cortex.

The result of you not trusting your own idea is that you set up a negative *click, whirr* or *like/dislike* response in the rest of the group. If you present an idea with nervousness or apprehension, you are actually signaling to the others that they should doubt your idea just as much as you do. They will respond with doubt and criticism; often not even aware as to why they feel that way. Children are much better at giving ideas without self-doubt because their dorsolateral prefrontal cortex—the brain's censor—hasn't fully kicked in yet. They doubt very little about what they do because the brain's critical-thinking system hasn't turned on. They simply don't know that their idea isn't perfect.

Adults, having had ample experiences of being told, "That will never work," are fully aware of their limitations. Having been criticized often enough, it is natural to want to protect one's ego by offering ideas with a caveat. These cover-my-backside tactics usually come in the form of, "This is just a thought..." or "I don't know if this will work..." or "Someone else may have a better idea..." We want everyone in the group to be aware that, if the idea proves to be foolish, we knew it right from the start. By the time adults get through these pre-idea warning phrases, we hate the suggestion before even hearing it. Children tend to switch the order of delivery. They get us excited *before* telling us the idea; "I've got an idea for a really cool game! Do you want to play?" Other kids end up wanting to play the game without even knowing what it is. The *click, whirr* and *like/dislike* processes have been used to their advantage. Next time you offer an idea, use them to your advantage.

Rule number two, *Don't Negate or Deny* deals with how the group plays together. We will discuss in more detail just how debate plays a role in brainstorming, but for now just keep in mind that *how* someone denies is just as important as *if* they deny.

The third rule, *Don't Ask Questions*, is also a topic of debate in the world of improvisation. Keith Johnstone is considered another founder of modern improvisation. He worked for the Royal Court Theatre in London in the late

1950s as Associate Artistic Director. In order to inspire more creativity from the actors, he developed what he called *improvisatory* exercises. Using these exercises during rehearsals proved to be a highly effective means of releasing the creative spirit of the actors. To everyone's surprise, those watching rehearsals found the improvisatory exercises as entertaining as the plays the actors were rehearsing. Johnstone took a chance and arranged a tour of universities throughout Great Britain to showcase his new creation. The new theatrical style was a hit.

Johnstone's art form became widely popular and his techniques are now taught around the world. His book, *Impro* describes the approach. Americans shorten *improvisation* to *improv*, Europeans shorten it to *impro*. (I think it's because we drive on opposite sides of the street.)

Rather than eschewing questions, as is taught in most American improvisation, Johnstone believes in the power of using open-ended questions. If an actor were to freeze up onstage with no idea what to say next (a common threat when there is no script), Johnstone would encourage the other actors to offer an open-ended question; "My God, what's that?" In improv, anything you say should be considered by your partner as perfect. Johnstone believes that asking a partner a question doesn't put any burden on them because any answer they give will be accepted without judgment. The answer—what-ever it is—is perfect and provides the new direction of the scene. In brainstorming, questions should simply be monitored to make sure the person isn't using them to either negate an idea, "How's *that* going to work?" or to avoid the responsibility of offering their own suggestions. If you know that someone in your group is just not the type that can create an idea (which is rare), you can use them to help flush out the ideas of others by asking leading questions. This allows them to be a valuable participant in a manner that supports their personality.

Stay Actional is an important rule for brainstorming. Brain research has been discovered that when a person engages in repetitive, rhythmic movement, the brain speeds up. Neural synapses connect more freely. Thinking flows more easily and ideas have a greater breadth of creativity. Rhythmic movement calms a person, releasing alpha waves and sparking brain activity. You might remember the last time you took a walk. A few minutes into this rhythmic, repetitive activity you started getting a headful of ideas. You couldn't wait to get home and write them down. The minute you got home and sat down, the ideas were gone. The chair soaked them up.

If you are conducting a brainstorming session while sitting around a table staring at each other, get ready for everyone to lose energy quickly. It is not to say that the brain can't work while seated; some of the most brilliant books (like this one) have been written while seated at a computer; but don't let a group go too long without movement.

Encourage people to pace, toss a ball back and forth; anything that inspires a rhythmic movement. Make sure the actions don't take concentration to perform (i.e. a jigsaw puzzle). These kinds of actions distract from the brainstorming. The movements should require no thought or concentration to perform.

Some people are not particularly kinesthetic, preferring to sit still so they can concentrate. These people, called auditory learners, prefer to shut down their body to avoid distraction. They often sit with their arms folded while thinking. Don't assume that an auditory learner is disinterested or uninvolved. Their physical signals can often be misinterpreted as negative when they are actually being thoughtful. A good facilitator will make sure everyone's style of thinking is supported. To get the best out of everyone, let the movers move and the non-movers sit and contemplate. This is not to say that auditory learners cannot benefit from rhythmic movement, but they may prefer to pace on their own rather that connect with others in a paired activity such as throwing a ball.

> *Inspiration isn't intellectual.*
> Keith Johnstone
> Author of *Impro*

The rest of the rules are self-explanatory, but—as with most group activities—preparing the individual is the first step to helping the group be successful. Now, let's discuss how to get the group ready.

Making Assumptions is a rule that is easier to follow for some than for others. Some people have been raised to believe everything they say has ultimate value. This may be frustrating when you are debating politics with them, but it is very valuable in brainstorming. If you have people in the group who don't fully believe what they say, you may have to discuss the *trust yourself* rule before continuing. Don't let people denigrate their own ideas simply because they aren't experts. The best ideas will often come from complete novices.

Give & Take may seem to suggest that everyone be asked to participate equally, but that isn't the goal. Onstage you will see improv performers who are silent for an entire scene, only to deliver the best line of the entire show at the end. *Give & Take* does encourage courtesy. Don't let the loudmouths take control such that the quieter folks feel shut out. But don't try to get an equal number of ideas from everyone, encourage give and take such that everyone participates at their own pace and comfort level.

Focus or *Listen, Watch, Concentrate* reminds a group that even one person who looks like he has "checked out" can be damaging to the momentum needed for brainstorming. Everyone should be as attentive to their partner's suggestions as they ask others to be for their own.

Work to the Top of Your Intelligence is one of my favorite rules because it is where the seat of creativity lies. As a professional speaker I am a member of the NSA, National Speakers Association. Professional speakers are keenly aware of how much scrutiny our profession endures, probably because of how many bad speakers there are in the country. There are many speakers who claim to be experts, and they really aren't. They deliver their presentations to snoozing audiences at conventions, thereby driving down the reputation of the entire industry. As such, members of the NSA are always encouraged to continually research their material and remain up to date. We are told not to be a speaker who has simply "read one more book than the audience." Brainstorming requires the same diligence, and the research should not focus solely on the product or service at hand. Maintaining a broad-based interest is necessary for developing creative and useful ideas.

CHAPTER 2

Preparing the Group

Preparing the person does little unless the group is also in the right frame of mine. It is a waste of time for an individual to suggest great ideas if the group is simply going to shoot them down. To properly prepare a group, the first step is to discard old notions of group dynamics. For generations, some people were labeled *creative* types and others *analytical*. Organizations often rely on the creatives to offer wild and innovative ideas, then hand the ideas to the analytics for implementation. This is a hold-over from the creation of the modern education system. Much of the educational process is a result of the Industrial Age. The chief goal of the Industrial Age was output; get as many widgets made in a day as possible. In order to produce good workers, the education system followed the same system of categorization as factories. Very early in life, a student was labeled according to a set of skills and educated as such.

This process may have served a nation looking for assembly-line workers, but it is terrible for innovation. It is also not an accurate way of looking at people. The result of the Industrial Age was a nation that instantly categorized people according to job title, school degree, or training certificate.

There is no such thing as a creative or non-creative person. There are only situations in which we either flourish or flounder. Tests conducted on people in creative professions (art, advertising, music) were compared to those from analytic professions (accounting, engineering, insurance). When it came to developing innovative solutions to problems, there was no difference in the output of any profession. Don't fall into the habit of categorizing people.

> *Specialization is for insects.*
> Robert Heinlein
> Author and philosopher

The Three Killers

I have identified what I believe are the three most common killers to personal or organizational success: Ego, Fear, and Complacency. At any given time, we all suffer from one or more of these emotions, and they lead to disaster.

Ego keeps people from trusting their partners. It destroys the positive atmosphere of lively debate and replaces it with defensiveness. This shifts the attention from the idea (where it belongs) to the person. Ego keeps people from remembering that the most important result is a good idea, no matter who came up with it. Ego places the needs of the self above the needs of the group.

Fear keeps the best ideas hidden inside where they don't do any good. Fear inhibits honest critique. Fear destroys a playful atmosphere; so instead of creativity-enhancing alpha waves, the brain goes into fight-or-flight mode. Fear is the most common culprit when a brainstorm session results in the same old safe ideas. Fear lives best in an atmosphere where status is everything. It is more important to avoid looking bad than it is to risk offering a potentially brilliant idea.

Complacency is the bad cousin of comfort. Extreme comfort leads to complacency, which leads to adherence to the status quo. Of course, the only reason to brainstorm is to challenge the status quo. Complacency can take the energy right out of a team. The first step of a good facilitator is to put these three words in front of the group; in bold letters write EGO, FEAR, and COMPLACENCY. Let the group know that is normal for each team member to suffer from one or more of these killers; which emotion they experience will depend on the day or the person. A good facilitator will keep a close eye on the team members for signs of ego, fear, or complacency. The best way to help a team member who is experiencing difficulty with these killers is to have a private conversation. Maintaining an atmosphere of safety is necessary for creativity, and public confrontation is inappropriate for all but the most comfortable teams. Talk about the signals that led you to thinking they were having difficulty and see if you are correct. The most important goal is to determine why they are feeling these emotions. It may be behaviors of the team that can be addressed or the cause might be external (a previous workplace that was oppressive, an argument at home). Most of the time, simply acknowledging the situation will do much to improve it.

Who to invite? Everyone!

The composition of the brainstorming team is vital, and most companies get this part wrong. Typically, only experts in the field are included, which—on the surface—seems to make sense. What is the point of inviting a grocery retailer to a discussion about computer software? As it turns out, it makes a lot of sense.

Jonah Lehrer tells a great story in his book *Imagine* about Dick Drew, a salesman at 3M in the early '20s. At that time, *Minnesota Mining and Manufacturing* (3M's name at the time) mainly sold sandpaper and other abrasives. Drew would visit auto body shops and demonstrate how well 3M sandpaper would work for sanding cars getting paint jobs. Occasionally, he would stay behind and watch the technicians work.

He noticed that the process for painting two different colors on a car was to glue paper to the car with an adhesive, paint the first color, tear off the paper, and then apply new paper in order to paint the second color. The problem was that the adhesive was so strong that it took a lot of paint off with it. As a result, the technicians ended up having to do a lot of touch-ups for every paint job. Drew knew that 3M used a variety of adhesives to make grit stick to paper to make sandpaper. So he set about experimenting with different glues to make one that would make paper stick to a car lightly enough that it wouldn't tear off the paint.

The story is much more involved and ended up with the creation of masking tape, Scotch Tape, and many other 3M products, but the point here is the resistance Drew received while working on the project. William McKnight was, Drew's boss and later became the CEO of 3M. Not seeing the immediate benefit of Drew's efforts, McKnight actually ordered Drew to cease his experiments. McKnight believed that, since Drew was a salesman and not a chemist, he should stick to selling. Drew believed in his idea so much that he kept working during his free time until he found success (and developed some the highest grossing products of all time).

People from entirely unrelated professions can yield creative solutions that elude industry professionals. Another story from *Imagine* involves Eli Bingham, Vice President of the drug company Eli Lilly. In the late 1990s, the company was experiencing a major hurdle in drug research. No matter how hard they tried, the scientists at Eli Lilly could not come up with a solution. Bingham had a crazy idea, ask people outside Eli Lilly to help solve the problem. In fact, open up the problem to scientists who weren't even trained in pharmaceuticals.

People told Bingham he was crazy. They said there was no way outsiders could fully understand the challenges of Eli Lilly. Bingham, however, looked at the situation more logically. Eli Lilly was spending a ton of money on the problem and they were not finding the answer. Going outside for help was really not the risk others thought it was. Against all advice, Bingham launched *InnoCentive*, a website that allowed companies to post challenges to problems and offer a reward for those who found the solution. Bingham's colleagues were aghast. He was literally posting company secrets for the world to see. Anyone could steal Eli Lilly's ideas. Instead, a remarkable thing happened. Solutions started pouring in from everywhere, and from the most unlikely sources. People were offering solutions for problems completely outside their own industry or field of study. Because people weren't hindered by their *already knowing*, they came at problems with a, "I'm no expert, but have you thought of this?" approach.

The site was so successful, it was spun off from its parent company and has, to date, be responsible for some of the most creative and profitable ideas for industries ranging from agriculture to mathematics. The only thing that makes this possible is the courage to invite an outsider's opinion and the willingness to listen. The advice of an answer may come at the expense of your ego. Very often, what outsiders see, and what you miss, is what you are doing wrong. I have actually had executives tell me they are afraid to ask for customer feedback because they are afraid of what they might hear. John Lehrer put it best when he wrote in *Imagine*, "[In order to be creative] you have to put aside your ego and listen to people who may not have nice things to say about you."

Allowing outsiders to offer suggestions resulted in a quick solution to a problem facing a group of high school teachers I was working with. I was asked to conduct a series of workshops to help teachers move away from a lecture-based format (boring and ineffective) to a more interactive teaching style. At one point during the series, I had the teachers divide into groups of three, making sure that each person in the group taught a different subject. I had each teacher share a learning objective they were working on and had the others in their group offer suggestions for interactive teaching methods.

As I walked around the room listening to each group, I passed by a table with three teachers; math, English, and music. They were laughing and giving each other high fives. When I asked about the celebration, the English teacher said, "My classes are working on vocabulary right now, which most students hate. I haven't been able to figure out how to help them memorize new words. Simple repetition just wasn't working, especially if they kids didn't really care about the new words. When I posed the problem to the group, Chester here (the music teacher) suggested I have the kids make up Rap or pop songs about each new word."

I explained to the teachers that music involves rhythm, repetition, and rhyme, all of which have been shown to increase retention. And, since they were using styles of music the kids liked, the teacher will experience less resistance (as long as you respect the less musically inclined in the group and give them a different exercise). What a simple solution; one that was only possible coming from someone not engulfed in the problem.

At first, this solution seems simple, but it took someone not knee-deep in vocabulary words every day to see an easier path to success. Brainstorming sessions must include people not familiar with your company, your systems, or your product. At *Stevie Ray's Improv Company*, we wanted to increase the number of students in our *School of Improv*. For our brainstorming session, we invited ten current students, ten former students, and ten people who had never heard of us or improvisation. As you might expect, the current students told us what we wanted to hear, the former students (these people were likely "former" because they were not satisfied with the class) told us things we didn't want to hear. The people who had never heard of us told us the truth. Dissatisfied people may have a truth to share, but it can be clouded by anger or frustration. Current members of the organization may have too much ego invested to be honest. Outsiders suffer from neither of these obstacles; they only say what they see.

In *Blink*, written by bestselling author Malcolm Gladwell, we learn about Paul Van Riper. Van Riper is a military tactician and the head of the Marine Corps University. Van Riper took a step sideways while analyzing military operations and tactics. He wanted to develop training that would enable military leaders to better handle the chaos of war. He soon realized that this was possible. War invited chaos, and it is unlikely one could exist without the other. Rather than try to tame an untamable beast, he decided to learn how to ride it better. So he and a group of Marine Corps generals flew to New York to visit the trading floor of the Mercantile Exchange. What better place to witness chaos?

Van Riper and the generals quickly realized that the exchange traders had something to offer the military. They took the traders to Governor's Island and had them play war games, and then to Quantico to engage in military exercises in actual tanks. The result was astounding. The traders excelled at every chaotic military exercise that was thrown at them. The marines realized that they were in the same business as these "overweight, unkempt, long-haired traders." The two groups formed a bond and both benefited from the experience. It took the generals putting aside their egos and allowing a group of "undisciplined" traders to teach them new techniques. And it took the traders putting aside the stereotypes they had about the military.

One last word about providing a good mix of people, don't bog down your invited outsiders with too much information about your company. There is a strong urge to fill everyone's heads with everything they "need to know" before participating. The very worth of outsiders is that they aren't saddled with too much knowledge. Turning an outsider into an insider is great for hiring a new employee, but it results in poor brainstorming results.

Developing an Improvisational Environment

I spoke earlier about the Rules of Improv and how they help a person improvise and be creative. There is one thing about rules that most adults forget, you have to agree on them *before* the game starts. Children rarely start a game without knowing what the rules are. "That tree is out of bounds and there are no touch-backs. Go!" However, most adults create silent rules that they keep them to themselves. "If one person in this group interrupts me, I am going to lose it!" After our secret rule is in place, we wait for someone in the group to break it, then we pounce. The poor person who is being admonished didn't even know about the rule in the first place.

Even if it seems obvious to you, talk about the little things before they become problems. How and when do you offer an idea? How do you offer critique? How long do we work before a break? Is everyone bothered when someone takes a call during the meeting, or is it just a few people who are offended? This may seem simplistic, but no matter what *you* want to happen during the meeting, everyone else is an adult who has the right to make decisions that are opposite of yours.

Once the rules have been agreed upon, if someone breaks a rule, no excuses are allowed. The offender must apologize so the group can move on. An apology consists of three parts:

1) "I'm sorry."

2) "It was my fault."

3) "What can I do to make up for it?"

Anything other than those three statements usually leads to making an excuse. Trust is destroyed. I first heard the rules for a good apology from Randy Pausch. While a computer science professor at Carnegie Mellon, Pausch was diagnosed with terminal cancer. A tradition among professors is to imagine what their very last lecture on Earth would be; for Pausch it was a reality. His final lecture was published as *The Last Lecture*.

Here is another rule, tell people they are only allowed to apologize once or twice. Usually, the best is once at the beginning, "Oh. I'm sorry. I didn't realize I was doing that. It's my fault so let me know what I can do about it." One more apology at the end of the discussion is fine, "Once again guys, my fault and I'm sorry." People who apologize more than twice actually make others more uncomfortable. Multiple apologies end up placing the burden on the other person to make everything okay.

Watch kids play. If one kid knocks another kid down they say they are sorry once, then everyone forgets about the incident and they get back to playing. This is another good lesson for adults. When someone apologizes, the rest of the group must forget about the mistake and move on. Adults are great at harboring resentments. No wonder we are terrible at playing together.

Kids are good at another skill necessary for a group to remain productive; they get moving. If one kid delays the game by too much yammering, the other kids will say, "Shut up and play!" This is not so much a criticism aimed at the yammering child, it is a reminder about the purpose of the gathering; to play. Kids always keep in mind that they have two hours until bedtime. They can either get something done or waste that precious time. Adults always have a *bedtime* looming (deadlines), but we often end up talking so much we never get started. If your team is stuck in a talkative stall, someone say, "Let's shut up and play!" It is a fun reminder of a trap we all fall into.

The reason kids get playing faster is because they are adept at stopping a game and inserting a new rule when needed. Watch a group of children playing and invariably you will hear, "Stop, new rule. The fence is out of bounds, now back to the game!" Adults fear mistakes so much that they talk and talk and never get started. Trust that, if the need arises, the group will create a new rule to handle any situation. Just get the game started.

Trust Your Partner

Under the *Trust* rule of improv, we talked about fully believing in your own idea so you don't present it poorly. The other half of the *Trust* rule is *Trust your partner*. When children offer an idea for a game, as soon as the child is finished describing the game he or she is met with a "yes" response from the others; "That sounds cool. Let's play!" Most adults respond to a new idea with, "How is *that* going to work?" or "We tried that once already." The phrase, "We tried that once already" should be stricken from use in every company and organization. That phrase never provides a good idea; it only kills the idea just offered. So here is a "new rule!" You are allowed to say, "The last time we tried that it didn't work. Let's talk about why." That statement fosters discussion, which brings about new solutions. Anyone who says, "We tried that once already" must apologize.

Being *In the Moment*

A Japanese master swordsman was attending a performance of *Noh Theatre* in old Japan. Noh is a highly stylized form of theatre and requires decades of training to master. The swordsman brought along his senior student. The performance featured a well-known Noh actor and the swordsman was especially eager to witness his performance. When the performance ended, the student asked his master what he thought of the play. The old man replied, "It was very impressive, I only saw the Noh master break focus once. I think he was distracted by an audience member in the front row who was moving about."

Martial arts and theatre both require the practitioner to be of clear mind, and to think only in the present. Thinking about past mistakes will likely cause one to make the same error again. Worrying about the outcome of an engagement (the future) will cloud the thinking and cause failure. In theatre this is called being *in the moment*; the Japanese call it *zanshin* or "remaining mind." It is the state where your mind is clear of distractions, allowing you to focus only on the task at hand.

After the audience left the Noh theatre, the swordsman—being rather famous himself—was invited to visit the Noh master backstage. When the swordsman complimented the actor on his performance, the Noh master replied, "Thank you. I lost zanshin only once when I allowed a man in the audience to distract me."

Brainstorming does not require hours of meditation, (and please don't bring a sword to the session. Boy, did I learn that the hard way). It does require turning off all the distractions and respecting your partners by focusing on the task at hand. One cool exception was when I was leading a brainstorm session. While we were brainstorming slogans, one guy pulled out his smart phone to download lists of synonyms that were very helpful.

Leave me alone!

Some people are not group thinkers. The chaos of voices and ideas bouncing around the room sends them into stress. Don't force these people to participate in a group session. It is a waste of your time and theirs. At a company where I was conducting a brainstorming session, one of the team members clearly fit this category. He shut down whenever there was a group meeting. So, we had him go to a quiet office and occasionally check back with the group when he got an idea or two to share. It was a perfect use of his skills without interfering with the group process. Just make sure you check on the guy. We had one fellow who made this claim and we discovered him later playing video games in his office. He tried to tell us that Xbox was helping him think creatively. No dice.

People trust the familiar, yet desire the novel

The axiom above is common in the marketing industry. Humans want a little bit of excitement within the safety of *the known*. If you want good work out of a group, establish an understanding that you expect, and value, the seemingly ordinary as well as the kooky crazy. Find a location that is exciting and new, but not so wild that people are uncomfortable in the environment.

The Three Zones

We live in one of three zones, or states of being. The first is the Comfort Zone. This is the zone we hear about the most. People say, "I need to get out of my comfort zone!" which translates into, "I'm bored." Few realize there is actual science behind the zones in which we live. Two researchers in the early 1900s, Robert Yerkes and J.D. Dodson were studying the effects of stress on learning. They developed the Comfort Zone model as well as the *Yerkes-Dodson Learning Curve*. For a brainstorming facilitator, it is crucial to understand which zone is best for creativity, and which will send your team into a tail-spin.

The Comfort Zone, where we live most of the time, is marked by three qualities:

1) High familiarity with your surroundings and the task at hand
2) High productivity
3) Low learning or creativity

Because the Comfort Zone offers very little opportunity for learning, we can remain productive for only a certain amount of time before we get bored. For the brain to spark into high gear, you must enter the next zone, the Risk Zone.

The Risk Zone involves doing something unfamiliar, so it is marked by:

1) Unfamiliarity

2) Low productivity.

3) A spike in learning and creativity.

A drop in productivity usually causes people stress because we are typically judged by our output. Being in the Risk Zone is only productive if the individuals are assured that they are not being judged on output, only participation.

The outer zone is the dangerous one, the Panic Zone. The Panic Zone is marked by one condition:

An immanent risk of the loss of something of value.

If we are about to lose something of value, we retreat to the safety of the Comfort Zone; and it will be a cold day in Florida if we ever risk leaving the Comfort Zone again. Staying in the Comfort Zone, with its low learning environment, eventually causes us to burn out and we either quit or become a R.O.A.D. warrior; **R**etired **O**n **A**ctive **D**uty.

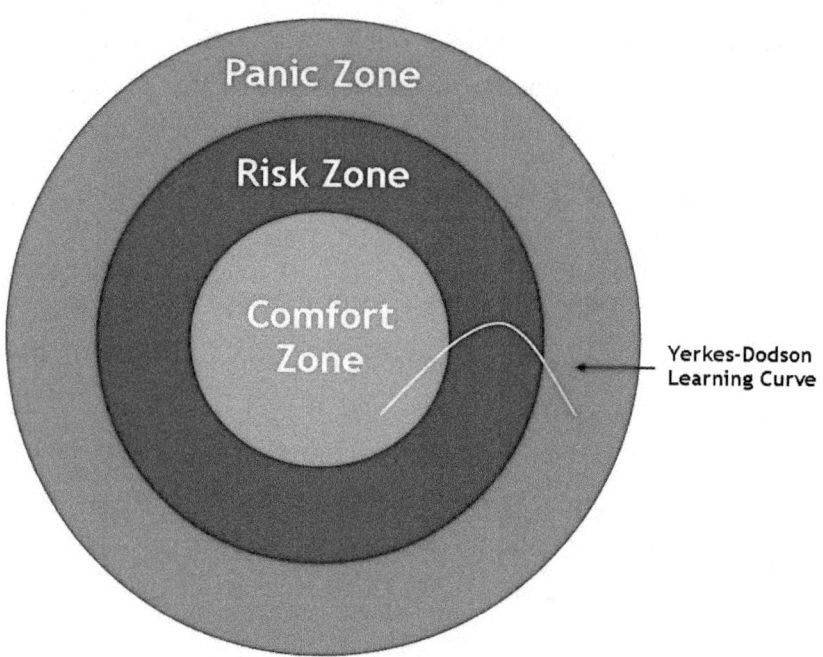

The thing a human being values most (after food, shelter, and plastic cling-wrap) is our self-image.

When psychologist Abraham Maslow developed his famous *Hierarchy of Needs* theory in 1943, the first level, *Physiological Needs*, was based on simple survival; food, water, and shelter. The next level is *Safety*, includes family, health, property, and employment. The third level is *Love & Belonging*; friendship, family, being part of a group. Fourth is *Esteem*; respect from peers. The highest level of needs is *Self-Actualization*; which includes morality, spirituality, creativity, acceptance of facts without prejudice (the last quality explains why most politicians never reach self-actualization).

Our self-image is engrained in almost every level. If working in a group threatens our self-esteem, we rarely seek to correct the problem, we retreat from it. Rarely does someone say, "My self-esteem is taking a hit here. Let's talk about it." Instead we get angry, uncooperative, or silent. You don't want team members retreating to the Comfort Zone only to eventually retire on active duty. This doesn't mean that people are fragile little eggs that can't take criticism, it just means that the facilitator has to monitor the process and make sure the debate stays focused on the idea and not the person who presented it. It is the worth of the idea at issue, not the worth of the team member.

Who is leading this pack anyway?

People, like all mammals, live on one of two states of being; a state of comfort or a state of nervousness. All emotions flow from one of those two states. A state of comfort leads to low stress, trust, likeability, creativity, and a desire to continue the activity. A state of nervousness leads to dislike, lack of trust, a fight-or-flight response, and a need to flee the environment. Extreme comfort can be as damaging as tension. Extreme comfort leads to complacency. People need a small amount of excited tension that doesn't explode into nervous tension. The excitement of "I wonder what will happen next?" is what makes for good brainstorming.

Dogs and humans react in many similar ways to stress or comfort, aside from chomping on slimy bones or licking places that shouldn't be licked. We are both calmed by a strong leader. Dog experts tell us that if you walk your dog and allow the pooch to walk in front of you, you are signaling that your dog is in charge. In the wild, when dogs walk in a pack, the alpha dog always walks in front to watch for danger. He or she is protecting the weaker dogs in the pack behind. If you walk behind your dog, you are signaling that he is the alpha and must protect the weak human behind it. This is why your dog might growl at other people or animals; it is not afraid or upset at the other animal, it is protecting you.

If, however, you hold the leash so the dog is slightly behind you, you will notice a marked change in the dog's behavior. Instead of him looking nervously from side to side to spot danger, he will fall into a steady loping walk. You have signaled that you are the alpha and he can relax.

A good brainstorming facilitator wants the group in a state of comfort, with just a twinge of excitement. The way to achieve this is to be the alpha dog. The alpha isn't pushy or demanding; rather, he is a protective leader. Many leaders believe that the purpose of their position is to tell others what to do. This is damaging and limits input. In traditional Asian companies, the manager actually feels responsible for any failure on the part of the workers. Instead of blaming the worker, the manager apologizes for allowing a situation to exist that would bring failure. Keith Johnstone, the founder of improvisatory theatre in England, would apologize to his students for any failure in his classes. He believed that their failure was simply a result of him not teaching correctly. I have a friend whose son attended post-secondary schooling. In one very difficult class, over ninety percent of the students failed a mid-term exam. Rather than blame himself, my friend's son went to class the next day and said to the teacher, "Boy, that many people failing must make you feel terrible." When the professor asked why, he replied, "One or two students failing means they didn't study. If ninety percent of the students fail, that means you didn't teach well." That's one gutsy kid.

No matter what happens, a good leader shows no fear and puts the group at ease with an, "I've got your back" attitude. If the facilitator shows apprehension or uncertainty, this creates a void of leadership. Any void in leadership must be filled, so someone else will take over. When this happens, it is rarely a smooth transition and the group is left wondering who is really in charge. Do your group a favor and be the alpha they want you to be.

The Power of Words

Take some time to talk to your group about word choice. This goes beyond the advice from mom, "If you don't have anything nice to say, don't say anything at all." In *The Happiness Hypothesis*, Jonathan Haidt cites clinical studies that tracked how people reacted to specific stimuli. In one test, people were asked to take a set of five words and use only four of them to create a sentence. Words like *they her bother see usually* could become *they usually see her* (leaving out the word *bother*). But the test was a trick. It wasn't really about people's ability to descramble words. The real test came afterwards. The subjects were told to finish the word test and then step into the hallway to talk to the experimenter. The situation was set up so that the experimenter would always be talking to someone else when the subject approached.

If the word test included words typically related to rudeness—*bother, brazen, aggressively*—the subjects would invariably interrupt the conversation. If the word scramble included words like *respect* and *polite*, the subjects would wait to be acknowledged, sometimes up to ten minutes. It turned out that, whether the words were read consciously or transmitted subliminally, the nature of the word affected the attitude of the subjects. If test subjects were exposed to words that related to the elderly, the subjects walked slower; words related to professors made subjects actually score higher in the game of *Trivial Pursuit*.

As far as human evolution goes, language and reasoning is a very recent development in the brain. Automatic responses have been around for tens of thousands of years longer than those higher-brain functions. This allows the automatic reactions quicker access to input and control over the brain. What this means to brainstorming is obvious; if you want good results you must consciously control the environment to avoid damaging subconscious reactions. Negative words will lead to negative outcomes, and most involved will not even be aware of it.

I believe that preparing a group goes beyond simply giving them the rules of the game and expecting a great outcome. You must educate people about what to expect and how *they might react to different situations. A discussion is* necessary about how the brain processes information; which is to say *not very well*. In *The Happiness Hypothesis*, Haidt explains more about this.

I discussed earlier that all brains have a built-in Approach/Withdraw Response. The brain senses input and immediately discerns the good stuff that we should approach (tasty food, a mate, a low-interest mortgage), and the bad stuff from which we should withdraw (a growling dog, a fall from high place, any Adam Sandler movie). This Like/Dislike switch runs constantly without our knowledge and has the greatest power over our behavior.

The challenge is that the Dislike/Withdraw reaction is faster and more powerful than the Like/Approach reaction. This is because the dislike part of the brain gets information first. All sensory input from the eyes and ears goes first to the thalamus, the central switching station in the brain. From there, the impulses are sent to sensory processing areas in the cortex, finally landing in the frontal cortex so you can actually think about what you just saw, heard, tasted, smelled, or touched.

What happens before the information gets to the frontal cortex? The amygdala (the fear/fight-or-flight part of the brain) grabs the input from the thalamus (it's okay, they live next door to each other) and reacts. The amygdala is not very good at signaling *everything is okay*. It much prefers fear because that is what kept humans alive to become the high-functioning creatures we are today who get conned into buying time-share properties in Burundi. Psychologists call this instant-withdraw reaction *negativity bias*.

Warn your group that negativity bias might compel them to instantly reject perfectly good ideas. Build in some time during the brainstorming session for thoughtful consideration so the frontal cortex can have time to work. Neural impulses move only about thirty meters per second, which means it takes a long time for input to get to the *thinking* part of the brain. You wouldn't want the amygdala to have the advantage just because it got first crack at ideas.

Status

We know that mammals are calmed by an alpha presence, which illuminates the importance of status in groups. Status can be damaging if not managed correctly. Gaps in status kill a playful, creative atmosphere.

I was conducting a brainstorming session in a company that was family owned. The patriarch was, to say the least, a piece of work. He knew everything and made sure you were aware of that fact. He started the company and spent thirty years building it, and was more than a little upset that his employees didn't show enough gratitude to him for "providing a decent living for them."

When the brainstorming session started, you could feel the tension in the room. As the facilitator, it was my job to make sure the session was productive, but Mr. Fun sitting in the back wasn't helping the process. He wasn't even doing anything that could be considered oppressive; just his demeanor was enough to take the energy out of the room.

So my first step was to level the playing field. To be fair, it wasn't my job to knock the man down or disrespect his position. He did, after all, spend thirty years building a great company. I would have preferred him to more congenial to his staff, but I wasn't his therapist or the staff's representative.

Leveling the playing field didn't mean bringing the boss down, it meant bringing everyone else up. I started by acknowledging what I call *the turd on the table* (some people call it the elephant in the room, but I think *turd on the table* is funnier). I addressed the entire group, "I know we all might be a little nervous because the big boss is right here and we want to do our best work for him, but he has assured me that he trusts each and every one of you and values what you bring to the table." I then looked at him with a sincere smile and said, "Right, sir?" At this point he had no other option but to agree. This was a powerful tool called *public commitment*. When people say something in front of a group, they are bound to follow through on their commitment. He publicly committed to respect everyone's input.

I continued, "Mr. X and I have also had many conversations about this process and he agrees that status can be an inhibitor when it comes to brainstorming, so he has decided to remove his *Boss* hat and play like everyone else." The first thing I did following that set-up was to have the group play a few whole-brain games. This inspired laughter, which is a great leveler of status. Rather than allowing the boss to sit and observe (the desired position for those who thrive on authority), I had him play along with everyone. The reason whole-brain games are a great leveling agent is that nobody is any better at them than anyone else. So Mr. Fun succeeded and stumbled as much as everyone else. That set the stage for a fun, productive, and stress-free session. A no-stress environment was certainly a breath of fresh air for the staff, and Mr. Fun actually discovered that communicating at the same level of his staff was much more satisfying than hovering above them.

When dealing with high-status people, I always try to remember that their biggest fear can be losing that status in front of the group. This would send them into the Panic Zone. I respect the fact that they worked hard to get where they are. I provide an environment in which their status is safe, but will not hinder the productivity of the group.

You're wrong! Let me tell you why

Another rule to establish when preparing the group is how disagreements will be handled. When the advertising executive Alex Osborn was first developing his rules of brainstorming in the 1950s, a cornerstone of his theory was that *no idea is a bad idea*. His assumption was that criticism inhibits creativity. This sounds logical, so most people took it at face value. Brainstorming has largely followed this rule since then. The problem with most assumptions is that research eventually disproves them; and such is the case for Osborn's rule against argument and criticism.

In *Imagine*, Jonah Lehrer cites numerous examples of how debate and criticism actually enhances creativity. When forced to defend an idea, a person's creative brain kicks into high gear and the idea is flushed out even further. Charlan Nemeth, a psychologist at UC-Berkeley, conducted a study involving teams of students who were told to brainstorm solutions to traffic congestion in the San Francisco Bay area. Some teams were given no guidelines and were allowed to develop ideas as they saw fit. Other teams were told to follow Osborn's rule and refrain from any criticism. They were to treat every idea as a good one. The third set of teams were told to toss out as many free-wheeling ideas as they could, but to debate and criticize each other's ideas as much as they wanted.

The results revealed that both groups that were given instructions slightly outperformed the no-instruction group. However, the teams that engaged in debate developed many more ideas than the no-debate group. When reviewed by industry experts, the ideas were deemed to be more creative and useful. Nemeth stated in her report, "While the instruction 'Do not criticize' is often cited as the most important instruction in brainstorming, it appears to be a counterproductive strategy. Our findings show that debate and criticism do not inhibit ideas, but, rather, stimulate them relative to every other condition." This all may seem to run counter to the rule of "yes, and" I described earlier, but the two concepts can indeed live in harmony. "Yes, and" does not actually call for complete agreement, it calls for cooperation. In fact, great improv can involve great disagreement. As long as the disagreement is conducted in a spirit of cooperation the group can remain productive.

As Jonathan Haidt explains in *The Happiness Hypothesis*, we develop judgments instantly. Whether the judgments are moral, social, or personal, we make decisions immediately and then look for reasons later. As Haidt puts it, "feelings come first, then reasons are invented on the fly." When we search for—or invent—reasons, our creative mind takes over. It is no wonder that having to justify a decision results in a greater breadth of ideas. Just think back to when you were eight years old trying to talk your way out of trouble with your parents. There is no greater jump-start to creativity than being put on the spot.

The late Steve Jobs used the debate strategy to heighten creativity at Apple, Inc. While ideas are kicked around at Apple, a debate session is built into the process. This has resulted in some of the most creative ideas the world of computers has ever seen. Structured critique sessions are also part of the corporate philosophy at creative companies such as Pixar Studios and Lucasfilm. Ed Catmull of Lucasfilm learned this philosophy from Toyota, where every person involved in the manufacturing process was charged with looking for errors. This brutally honest approach causes some to fear that a derisive atmosphere will result, but it actually enhances trust. When people are honest with you, you know they aren't hiding anything. And, if you discover their objections do indeed hold no water, the debate has still flushed out more ideas. As Lehrer states, "Dissent, event when wrong, expands creativity."

Shut up so I can interrupt you!

No discussion about group dynamics would be complete without including gender differences. A few decades ago there was a movement to try to convince people that men and women were exactly the same—except for some internal plumbing. Thankfully, we have moved back to the land of reality and now recognize—and embrace—gender differences. (And wouldn't the world be a boring place without them?)

As I mentioned before, you want just the right amount of stress in the process. This excitement is productive, as long as it doesn't turn into nervous tension. Men and women handle stress differently. When under stress, all humans produce an excess of cortisol. Cortisol is a regulatory hormone that is fine in normal amounts. Too much cortisol causes ill-temper, stress-related illness, and—in extreme cases—a shortened life-span.

Humans subconsciously seek out behavior to lower cortisol and mitigate stress. Men and women achieve this in markedly different ways. A study was conducted in which men and women were tested engaging in different behaviors, their blood was tested to see when cortisol lowered the most. Women lowered cortisol the most when they raised oxytocin. Oxytocin is a calming hormone (it is one of the three hormones given to induce labor). Oxytocin calms men too, but men don't produce it naturally.

When the tests were complete, it was discovered that women produce oxytocin the most whenever they engage in an activity that involves sharing. In fact, a separate study was conducted in which men and women were each given a sum of money to do with as they pleased. Half the group (which included both genders) was given an inhalant of oxytocin. At the end of the study, those who inhaled the hormone had no money. They had all shared it in some fashion or another.

This fact of physiology affects the communication style of women. Female communication is very detail-oriented because detail enhances sharing. Women tend to share reward. When given a compliment, women will usually respond by mentioning others who helped accomplish the task; thus sharing the reward. However, oxytocin isn't the greatest drug ever produced. Elevated levels can increase distrust in others and a territorial attitude. Just like most things, too much of a good thing isn't good.

Men must also reduce cortisol. The behavior study determined that men reduce cortisol the most when they produce testosterone. Testosterone is produced most in males when they engage in any act of taking credit for an accomplishment. This explains a lot; like why, when a man empties the dishwasher, he acts like he built an addition on the house. Women will say, "I emptied it twelve times. What do you want, a medal?" The answer is, yes we do.

An accomplishment-based creature cannot simply share in a household chore, that doesn't equate an achievement or raise testosterone. Men must create an accomplishment out of an everyday activity. And, sadly, men must also deny failure. Failure, being the opposite of accomplishment, is quite damaging to a male.

Men and women do best when they recognize what the other needs and give it to them. Men must listen when women speak, even if there is more detail than men want; remembering that the importance is on the person, not the event. Women must remember to praise, even if the act seems trivial. While facilitating a brainstorming session, men must be monitored when it comes to interrupting. Men interrupt women far more often because listening is not an accomplishment, talking is. Females usually provide more support in communication; they nod their heads more frequently during conversation to show attention, they engage in more eye contact, they utter "uh huh" and "I see" more often than males. To provide a productive, stress-free brainstorming environment, make sure females are in a sharing environment. Allow them to share all the details of their ideas. Allow males to accomplish by focusing criticism on the idea itself, not the person delivering it.

Come on, this is serious

Let's talk about how fun and laughter fit into the process. Ask any employee what their first assumption is when they hear people laughing at work and they will say, "They must not be getting any work done." This long-held bias against joy in the workplace is, fortunately, beginning to fade, but not fast enough. The belief that laughter and productivity are mutually exclusive came from age-old misguided attitudes. This assumption is based on the assumption that, if you are focusing on laughing with your friend you can't be focused on work.

An example of assumption without fact is the Ford Motor Company. Henry Ford is widely regarded as the inventor of the assembly line. In fact, the assembly line dates back to ancient China; the famous Terra Cotta army was constructed in an assembly line process. Ford used the method to increase production at the Ford Motor Company. Ford was not known to be a friend of the working man; in fact, he was constantly suspicious that any employee would cheat him if given the chance. Ford instituted a policy at the plant in which smiling was a disciplinary offense. If a manager caught you smiling, you obviously weren't concentrating on your work. Laughing on the job could easily get a man fired. The adage, "You are here to work, not to have fun" ruled the plant.

Because Ford was one of the first to modernize the assembly line process, and his plant experienced—what was for the time—incredibly high production. Business leaders considered him a genius. Mistaking coincidence for cause-and-effect, many followed his lead concerning laughter in the workplace. This left the country with a legacy of fear and oppression in the workplace. Thankfully, research has shown that not only was Ford incorrect, but—when it comes to laughter— his assumption was the opposite of reality. Laughter actually improves hand-eye coordination. Assembly lines rely on perfect timing and coordination. If Ford had been privy to this information, he might have reversed his rule and *demanded* more laughter at the plant.

Laughter has long been known to improve physical health—easing pain, releasing healthy endorphins, lowering blood pressure—modern medicine has advanced to the stage where we can study how laughter affects the brain. Dr. Robert Provine, a professor of psychology and neuroscience at the University of Maryland-Baltimore County, has researched the effects of laughter on the human intellect for over two decades. His research has discovered that laughter actually causes the brain to speed up. Neural synapses fire more quickly during laughter.

Immediately following a *laughter episode* (usually lasting about fifteen seconds) a person can more easily solve complex problems, with a greater breadth of ideas. This is likely because laughter causes more centers of the brain to cross-communicate than any other form of communication. Laughter also de-stresses the brain, which enhances creativity. In *Imagine*, Lehrer cites the work of Mark Beeman, a scientist at the National Institutes of Health. Beeman studied laughter and its impact on problem solving and creativity. Beeman discovered that people who scored high on a standard measure for happiness solve about twenty five percent more insight puzzles than those who are angry or upset.

Laughter engages the highest centers of the brain—language, critical thinking, discerning meaning and incongruity, and comparative thinking. A laugh-filled life has even been connected to higher IQs. Laughter also provides another benefit for the working environment. People produce better when they are fully engaged in their task instead of watching the clock. The brain's internal clock can greatly inhibit creativity. You know this if you ever begin a task close to the end of the work day. You want to say, "Let's just leave this until tomorrow."

Laughter automatically engages what psychologists call *time distortion*. Time distortion is when your internal clock turns off and time flies. This happens when you are so focused on the current activity that you don't care about the outside world; watching a great movie, listening to a compelling speech, or watching a good play. Tell a group of playing children that it is time to get ready for bed and

77

their first response is, "We just started the game!" They could have been playing for hours, but—to them—the game just started. This is because laughter stopped the clock.

Provine's research also discovered that children laugh an average of 200-300 times per day. Women laugh 196 percent more than men, but men create more laughter in conversation. Part of Provine's study involved having research assistants track social laughter as opposed to laughter in a theatre or comedy club setting. These assistants would act as fly-on-the-wall observers in shopping malls, parties, and other public gathering places. They utilized a method to chart the laughter they observed. Whenever laughter occurred, they would chart who instigated it, what was said, who was the listener/audience, and the situation in which the laughter occurred. Males tend to laugh more when speaking with male counterparts, and females laugh more when they are the ones speaking. This will play out in a brainstorm session, depending on the familiarity of the group. Female laughter during speaking can either be a signal of conviviality or of nervousness. If you witness nervous laughter, creativity may be inhibited and you should play a status-leveling activity before moving on.

Remember the last brainstorm session that seemed to drag on forever? It is likely that laughter was absent. It is crucial for a facilitator to *plan* for laughter; to monitor the atmosphere of the room and place strategic laughter breaks. Continual laughter is obviously not the goal either. Too much laughter causes a loss of focus. Laughter should be used as a *brain break* for those moments when everyone is stuck for ideas or the energy is lagging.

In order for laughter to be productive, it must be shared. All of human laughter can be divided into two categories: *reward* or *reprimand*. The only other animal capable of laughter is the chimpanzee, which only laughs during rough play or when tickled. The *Laughing Hyena* is not actually laughing, its bark only sounds like a laugh. We laugh *with* someone to reward; in agreement of something they said, or when they accomplish a task like sinking a basketball. We laugh *at* someone to show them they are acting like a fool. In this case, laughter is a tool to keep humanity in line.

The trouble is that the fear of being laughed *at* diminishes creativity. Acting out of the ordinary may bring creative results, but you risk the derisive laughter of your peers. Most people prefer to fit in and be ordinary than to risk being seen as goofy. As Keith Johnstone states in *Impro*, "Laughter is a whip that keeps us in line. It is a horrible thing to be laughed at against your will. Either you suppress unwelcome laughter or you start controlling it. We suppress our spontaneous impulses, we censor our imaginations, we learn to present ourselves as 'ordinary', and we destroy our talent—then no one laughs at us."

When planning strategic laugh breaks, don't try to create situations where people have to *be funny*. Over ninety percent of laughter is not the result of something funny being said. Laughter is most often the result of people sharing experiences. People are sixteen times more likely to laugh at something if they are in a group than if they experience the same thing alone. This is because we laugh when we share experiences. (If you are sitting around laughing by yourself, we need to get you some help.) If your group needs a laugh break, get people talking about anything except the task at hand; or play a whole-brain game. Allow the group to share or play and laughter will take care of itself.

Can't you find anything good to say?

Every group has one; the person who hates every idea. These people can be a drain on the fun, the creativity, and the energy. It can sometimes feel like the only solution is to hold the meeting in secret without telling them, but it is helpful to first understand the nature, and the biology, of a pessimist.

In reality, all humans are pessimists whether they know it or not. Because the brain's most important goal is to keep its host body safe, it spends a lot of energy on the look-out for danger; real or perceived. That is why it is easier to frighten people into action than it is to lure them into it. In fact, the brain has twice as many receptors for negative input than it does for positive input. This is the product of thousands of years of evolution, most of which we humans had to spend avoiding danger.

The imbalance of negative vs. positive receptors causes even neutral input to be skewed negative. If you say to someone, "Hey, you got a haircut" they will often perceive the comment as a criticism, rather than a neutral statement. They might respond with, "Why? Does it look stupid?" A neutral comment like, "I see you wore gray today" might be met with, "That's okay, isn't it?" The level of negative bias depends on the person and the circumstance. During brainstorming, this phenomenon can cause ideas to be instantly judged negatively. It can also cause an over-reaction to criticism (unless the group has a good foundation of trust).

Even a pessimist can be of benefit during brainstorming. Past successes can cause some to become lazy and overconfident. A bit of what psychologists call *defensive pessimism* can help us imagine potential hazards and pitfalls. Developing solutions for potential problems will ultimately lead to a successful outcome, but only if you have a healthy level of pessimism to be on the lookout.

Lawrence Sanna, a University of Michigan psychology professor says, "The interesting thing about people who engage in defensive pessimism is that they tend to be quite dynamic and successful. They use the technique to motivate themselves to do the very best job they can." Another University of Michigan professor, Edward Chang, states, "The phenomenon of defensive pessimism shows that there are times when pessimism and negative thinking are actually features of positive psychology, since they lead to better performance and personal growth."

As long as the *Negative Nelly* in the group fully participates by offering suggestions and helping to solve the problems she identifies, negative thinking can help lead to a positive outcome.

I'm too young to learn anything new

The statement above was actually uttered to a friend of mine. My friend, Dave, is an Emergency Room physician I met while in college. I worked my way through school as an ER Assistant on the night shift. Dealing with blood and trauma from 12:00-8:00a.m. made going to freshman English seem even more boring than usual. Dave loves to keep up on all the modern research in medicine. You would think that all doctors would be glued to medical journals for up-to-date procedures and new protocols, but this is not always the case. This knowledge gap can be a problem in the medical profession.

In some hospitals, ER doctors are seen as little more than glorified medics. They must often defend their decisions to physicians from other departments; especially if the new doctor is taking over the care of the patient in question. Dave was being challenged by a younger resident for using a protocol that was not standard procedure. When Dave cited evidence for the new protocol from the Journal of the

American Medical Association (a doctor's Bible), the resident shook his head and said, "I'm too young to learn anything new." Dave stared in disbelief as the resident wheeled the patient away on the cart, to what fate we will never know.

The issue of age and generational differences has become more intense in the past few years because there are more age groups in the workplace now than at any time since child labor laws were first created. When an economy dips, older folks are forced to put off retirement, which results in an aging workplace. Advances in medicine also keep people alive longer. Those people want to stay productive. Currently, it is possible to have four generations in the same company; *Traditionalists*, *Baby Boomers*, *Generation X*, and *Generation Y*. When *Generation Z* becomes old enough to work, we may see five generations working side by side. Imagine the conversations. "You mean you had to get up off the couch to change the TV channel?!" If medical advances continue to lengthen life spans, the phrase, "The boss is, like, two hundred years old!" will be more fact than exaggeration.

Check out the charts on the following two pages and you will see the conditions that affect different age groups. These conditions affect how that generation might respond to a facilitator (attitude toward authority) or a fellow team member (job value). The Traditionalist Generation was taught by their parents that, "You don't have to like your job, you just have to have one" as well as "You don't have to like your co-workers, you just have to work with them." The advice of "Leave your home life at home when you come to work" was borne out of the instability of the Great Depression. You did whatever you could and withstood whatever hardship was necessary to put food on the table.

Even though some of these work ethics have recently been discovered to decrease productivity and reduce longevity, they are still firmly held beliefs among certain employees and can affect teamwork during brainstorming.

Generation	Traditionalists	Baby Boomers	Generation X	Generation Y
Birth Years	1925-1945	1946-1964	1965-1980	1981-1999
Conditioning Years	1930s-1940s	1950s-1960s	1970s-1980s	1980s1990s
World Frame	Depression, WWII Struggle/sacrifice delayed gratification	Sexual revolution, economic expansion, abundance, spending	MTV, AIDS, cynical, grim economy	Blur between tech/media and fantasy/reality, Great Recession, tech in pockets
Family Structure	Nuclear	Divorce	Latch-key Kids	Friends become family
Who is Trusted	Doctors	Feelings	Technology	Internet
Music	Swing, Big Band	Rock & Roll, New Age	Rap, Punk, Alternative	Hip Hop, Gangsta
Authority	Respect it	Question it	Challenge it	Non-hierarchal

Generation	Traditionalists	Baby Boomers	Generation X	Generation Y
Work Ethic	Pay your dues, keep your head down, "I am my job."	Climb the ladder, workaholic, "Work is my life."	Only 9-5, independence, "Work gives me a life."	Work isn't everything, "I have a life outside of work."
Management Style	Command & control	Collaborative	Entrepreneurial	Collaboration
Loyalty to	Company	Profession	Family	Friends
Job Value	Stability, security	Career growth	Stepping stone	Parallel career paths
Communication	No news is good news	Any news is good news	Need news	Instant feedback
Resents	Change, lack of respect	Control, slackers	Corporate politics, seniors clogging the system	Rising crime, adherence to tradition
Values	Stability, loyalty	Variety, achievement	Learning, quality of life	Freedom of choice, diversity

It has long been assumed that age affects creativity. The older you get, the more stuck in old patterns you become. However, modern research has discovered that the brain is not a fixed organ, wired at birth for a lifetime of a certain kind of thinking. The mind is a fluid organism that can be retrained, rewired, and constantly improved. Although cognitive abilities may begin to diminish as you get older, age has little to do with creativity. Age can, however, affect the group dynamic. What is respected (authority vs. personal freedom) will have an impact not only the ideas presented, but the manner in which they are received. In years past, a younger employee would be told to "sit back and watch the masters at work," but that attitude risks having the best ideas sit silent as well.

I have been asked many times to help facilitate idea sessions where management was trying to gain greater cooperation between the older and younger generations. The problem is, the younger folks who are asked to attend are sat in the back of the room and no one listens to them. This isn't the best way to build bridges. On the other hand, I facilitated a wonderful workshop for a 4-H group. 4-H is an organization over 100 years old. It strives to develop youth into productive adults by enhancing their **Head**, **Heart**, **Hands**, and **Health**. This particular chapter realized that the adult leaders had, in a way, hijacked the club away from the kids. So, at the meeting I conducted, the adults told the kids they would be in charge and be able to tell the adults exactly what kind of organization they wanted. It was hard for the older and wiser adults to keep quiet at times, but when they did they came away with some great new initiatives.

The information for the generational charts came from myriad sources. If you manage Generation Y employees and want to get the most out of that age group, check out the book, *Y in the Workplace: Managing the "Me First" Generation* by Nicole Lipkin and April Perrymore. These two psychologists take an objective look at the benefits as well as disadvantages of the mindset of a Gen Y worker. It is a refreshing change from the "What's wrong with kids these days?" dialogue you usually hear. If you do experience some obstacles due to generational differences, show everyone the charts above. Sometimes just seeing in print the stereotypes of their own generation will cause team members to be aware of their own behavior. And awareness is half the battle.

Explanation vs. Intuition

Like generational differences, the acceptance or denial of intuition can also affect a group. There are those who want answers for everything before the first step is taken. Any foray into the unknown is frightening for them. Perhaps they were chastised for every mistake while growing up, or came from a previous workplace where simple missteps were career-ending moves. On the other hand, there are those who hate to do their homework, preferring to rely solely on intuition. Any challenge to their suggestion is perceived as a personal attack.

The *Six Sigma* process proved effective at reducing waste in manufacturing, saving companies millions of dollars in cost overruns and lost productivity. Some Six Sigma champions thought, "Hey, let's use the same process in the design and creation phase of product development." This spawned *Design for Six Sigma*, or DFSS.

With this new system, employees who wanted to bring a new idea to the table would have to complete the DFSS matrix for the idea. This amounted to asking someone to have the idea completed before bringing it to others for consideration. Some engineering types loved this new development; it kept the weirdo's from introducing ideas that weren't fully flushed out. The problem is that this process completely destroys any intuition.

Companies, like countries, often allow the pendulum to swing too far in either direction. Complete adherence to structure prohibits crazy ideas, which is where market-disruptive ideas come from. On the other hand, a "just trust me, it will work" attitude skips over the hard work necessary to make an idea into reality. A total reliance on intuition can gloss over possible pitfalls, creating problems down the road. When all is said and done, there is no way to guarantee that an idea will work. Some amount of intuition is necessary for the all-too human process of brainstorming to bear fruit.

When my business partner, Pamela, is directing our improv troupe, she must often deal with a major part of the show; the Blackout. During one of our shows, an improv scene is done when the technical director running the sound and lights hits the switch and blacks out the stage lights. The black-out cues the audience that the improv is over. The audience applauds and the troupe is on to the next improv piece.

In comedy, timing is everything. The decision of when to black out the lights and end an improv is an awesome responsibility. Technicians-in-training will tell you it is the scariest moment during the show because if they black out the lights too soon, the improv falls short. The errant technician just killed any possibility of the scene becoming great. If the improv piece keeps going and going and going without a merciful black out to end it, the technical director can plan on hearing some very unkind words from the troupe after the show. (Blacking out too late is more common because hitting the black-out switch can be so frightening that some technicians simply let the improv keep going.)

While training new technical directors, Pamela has a saying that helps them understand how to take the leap, "Sometimes you have to close your eyes and pull the switch." The resulting black-out choice may be disastrous, but staying in one spot will kill you anyway. The same is true for brainstorming, sometimes you have to close your eyes and pull the switch. The results may be less than stellar, but staying in one place is the best way for a company to go bankrupt.

Leap and the net will appear.
　　　　　　　　　　　Zen saying

CHAPTER 3

Preparing the Space

There is a feeling among some facilitators that once you have "the right butts in the seats," the rest will take care of itself. However, properly preparing the individual and the group gets you only part of the way. A good brainstorming session is ultimately about creativity, and the physical environment has a definite impact on the outcome. If you want lots of out-there ideas, you have to have just the right amount of stimuli in the room. Remember the last time you sat in a cold, gray room while somebody said, "Who has got an idea?" Are you kidding?

Without the proper environment, creativity can be a struggle. There are two main elements to space:

1) Where you hold the meeting.

2) What is in the room.

Get out of Dodge!

Attitude plays an important role in creativity. If you shuffle people into the same old room day after day, their energy will wane. In fact, in order to get the best work out of the group, you want them to feel a bit pampered. That is why retreats work so well. Get away to a fun and energizing location (especially if you want people to focus on brainstorming instead of running back to their desks every twenty minutes to check on an "important e-mail").

In *Imagine*, Jonah Lehrer tells the story of Pixar executive John Lasseter needing an emergency fix for the movie *Toy Story 2*. The first draft of the movie was lackluster, and Lasseter had to act quickly. He arranged an emergency off-site summit of the movie's creative team. Simply meeting in an unfamiliar location made the team "outsiders" to their own project. In a neutral location, they were able to look at the project with fresh eyes.

When looking for a good space, try for a balance of energy. The grounds for the headquarters of 3M in Minnesota offer wooded trails and ponds for employees to stroll and rejuvenate (fostering alpha waves in the brain). However, you don't want the entire experience to feel like a Zen monastery. In studies cited in *Imagine*, it was discovered that large cities churn out more creative ideas than small towns. This is because, in seemingly chaotic environments, people bounce off each other in energizing and productive ways. Chance meetings result in random conversations. Random conversations can be just as effective as planned meetings in creating effective solutions.

In your day-to-day work environment, keep people moving around the office and running into each other in unplanned ways. In a planned brainstorm session, have moments of quiet reflection coupled with energizing chaos. In planning the offices of Apple in California, Steve Jobs designed random connections into the very building layout. He demanded that the only restrooms be on the main floor; forcing anyone who needed a bathroom break to walk to the same common area. At first this caused frustration among the staff, but later they discovered that some of their best ideas came from random encounters with other staff members on the way to the restroom.

Where are the toys?

In order to be creative, you need to be surrounded by stuff. The ratio of stimuli to creativity is a simple bell curve. As shown below, with no stimuli in the environment there is no creativity. As stimuli is introduced (photos on the wall, gadgets to play with, music and color) creativity improves. However, too much stimuli distracts the brain and causes a drop in creativity.

Creativity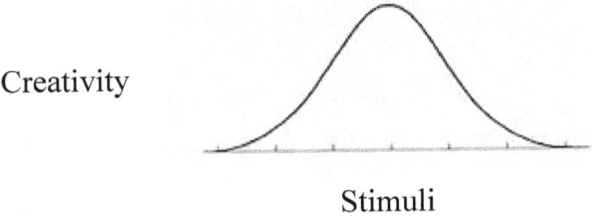

Stimuli

If you are stuck in a room that only has flat, gray walls, bring in posters or photos. They don't have to relate to the subject of the brainstorming; in fact, it would be better if they didn't. And since repetitive, rhythmic movement spurs brain activity, have balls for playing catch. Whatever you provide for the group, just make sure the toys don't take concentration to play; the brain will then focus on the game instead of the brainstorming.

Studies have shown that, while the color red improves concentration for tasks such as proofreading and analytics, the color blue provides for a much more creative environment. In the 1960's, Marian Diamond, a psychologist at US-Berkeley, discovered that an "enriched environment," including colors, sound, and physical stimulation provided for development of a larger and more complex brain. No wonder the modern workplace cubicle is leading people to say they are "brain dead."

A little something for everyone

People have different needs when it comes to engaging higher brain function, and a good facilitator will supply what each type of person needs. In general, people can be divided into a learning group based on the five major senses.

Since the visual cortex is the most efficient means of sensory input, most people respond best to visual stimulation. The room should have a variety of images and colors to keep this cortex alert. Some people are kinesthetic; they have to move. Don't force these people to sit for long periods of time. Have objects or gadgets handy to keep them occupied. Movement helps their brains connect ideas together. Others are aurally stimulated; they process primarily through sound. It is common for these people to shut down their bodies in order to concentrate. Movement is not only a distraction for auditory folks, but it can be frustrating. They often sit with their arms folded so they can concentrate.

Does someone in your home or at work like scented candles or potpourri? Olfactory types need a pleasing aroma to relax and think. Make sure the room doesn't smell sterile or have that just-scrubbed ammonia smell. And finally, guttural thinkers like to munch while contemplating. Have munchies available for them.

While we're on the subject, let's close out this section talking about food. Food may be sustenance, but it also feeds the soul. Humans consider food a reward. You don't have to have fancy food, but put some thought into it. Forget the plastic serving tray filled with granola bars or the bagels-and-fruit special from the local shop. People need to feel pampered, rewarded. Find some interesting and tasty treats for breaks and your group will feel like you care. They will reward you with extra effort, and great ideas. If possible, have people bring in homemade dishes and treats to share. Preparing food for someone else has always been a primal message of care and thoughtfulness. Taking a little time to cook shows your teammates you value them.

PART II

The Eight Steps

The reason most brainstorm sessions fail is not a lack of creativity, but a lack of structure. Too much effort is placed on the actual *brainstorming* without proper set-up or follow-through. The following eight step process was developed in conjunction with Gary Jader, my colleague and former board member. The steps must be followed in their order otherwise you will short-circuit creativity and achieve only average results. Before we jump into the first phase, however, let's remember that brainstorming doesn't only happen during the meeting. Creative professionals are never far from a notepad or digital recorder. I can't tell you how many million dollar ideas are floating in the atmosphere because I told myself I would write them down when I got back to the office. My wife is tired of watching T.V. with me because every other commercial for a new product has me saying, "Hey. I thought of that years ago." Of course, memory does play tricks on you as you age.

Back when I used to teach fledgling stand-up comedians, I would warn them that their best material would come while driving or doing mundane activities (when alpha waves are at their highest). In the comedy business we call these moments *spontaneous creation*, as opposed to sessions of disciplined writing. Spontaneous creation can make up the majority of a professional comedian's act, but Louis Pasteur said, "Chance favors the prepared mind." Brainstorming should be an ongoing state of mind.

One reason 3M is able to continually introduce groundbreaking ideas is because innovation is an expectation, not a chance occurrence. For years, 3M has followed a *Fifteen Percent Rule*. All of the scientists and researchers at 3M are expected to spend fifteen percent of their time working on projects with no clear outcome. The belief is that consistent attention to creative thinking will always be rewarded with usable products and 3M has the track record to prove it. One interesting addition to the fifteen percent rule is that 3M staff members are expected to share their ideas with a wide cross-section of fellow employees. Projects in the hamper that are kept a secret rarely result in a finished product.

CHAPTER 4

Laying the Foundation

The first question I ask clients during the getting-to-know-you meeting is, "Why do you want to have a brainstorm session in the first place?" This is usually met with a blank stare and a, "Because." The reason for needing new products and services might seem self-evident, but you have to understand your objectives in specific detail or you quickly run into problems. Properly handling the beginning stages of the process is important if you want success further down the road.

The first two steps of the innovative idea process fall into the phase called, *Laying the Foundation*. An essential beginning to brainstorming is to have absolute clarity about the organization; namely, why do you exist? I asked the "Why do you exist?" question to a medical device company that had hired me to help with team management and productivity. There were 1400 employees gathered for an all-company meeting. I had the employees sit in groups of four and told them to answer the question, "What is the one reason this company exists?" I also told them they couldn't use the company's mission statement. I love adding that condition. Half the people in the room roll their eyes because I just took away their easy answer. I think I missed my calling to be the high school teacher everyone hated.

After a few minutes, I asked the group to share some of their responses. One four-some said, "To save lives." Another said, "To achieve zero defects in our medical devices." Other answers included, "Become known as the best medical device company in the world," "Beat our competition," and "Provide maximum shareholder value" (guess who was in that group). Judging by the nature of the answers, you can guess the make-up of each group; sales, manufacturing, marketing, and administration.

All of the answers above are fine, but there is a problem; they aren't the same. Every employee within a company — from the CEO all the way to the mail room—must have the same answer to the question, "Why do we exist?" Even the slightest variation will cause a problem; not necessarily right away, but eventually. Things may run smoothly at first because employees will simply be performing their assigned duties. Sooner or later, however, there will be a disagreement. Every team eventually gets caught up debating which ideas to accept and which to reject. When teams get caught up debating over what to do next, there are only two ways to break the stalemate; 1) let the boss decide, 2) decide which suggestion best serves the *one reason the company exists*. There are plenty of fabulous ideas that can be discarded because they belong with a different company or organization. They don't support the *one reason you exist*.

For the medical device company, the goal of *zero defects in manufacturing* might aid in the goal of *saving lives*, but the goals are slightly different. One focuses on process, the other on the eventual outcome. Likewise, the goal of *becoming known as the best in the industry* involves the image of the company. Making image the primary goal of the organization would lead to different decisions than the goal of saving lives. If *providing shareholder value* is the ultimate goal, some defects in manufacturing might actually be considered acceptable. A cost-benefit analysis might lead to the decision of leaving equipment as is rather than conducting expensive upgrades.

The *one reason you exist* might frustrate some departments within a company because it might seem that the function of their priority a low priority. This problem can be mitigated if leadership clearly demonstrates how every function within the organization supports the *one reason*. During the eight step process itself, there will be plenty of debates. It is a lot easier to solve debates if you are able to say, "Carl, your idea is good, but it leads to more of an image outcome. Since Chad's suggestion connects more directly with the reason we exist, we're going to go with his idea."

The *one reason* should not be simply repeating the mission statement of the company because the two are slightly different. A company's mission statement is usually a complete declaration of what a company does and who it serves. Knowing this mission is vital to a company, but mission statements are usually filled with language that people don't use on a regular basis. The *one reason* should be something you could easily say to someone over coffee. Imagine sitting down with someone and having them ask, "So, what does your company do?" If your response was, "We effectively gather resources on behalf of our clients and allocate those resources to the benefit of residents within the seven county metro area" I don't think your friend would want to have coffee with you anymore.

The answer above was an actual statement by a participant at a workshop I was conducting for one of the county departments in my metropolitan area. This group was responsible for collecting child support payments from parents, as well as state agencies, to make sure the basic needs of the child were met. After some discussion about the *one reason* they existed, they amended their statement to, "We feed the babies." Their new statement was perfect because it contained an important quality in the *one reason*, emotion. Most mission statements illicit the same emotional response as the ingredient label on a jar of dog food.

When we conducted the brainstorm session for our *School of Improv*, Gary Jader was part of the group. I stood up and immediately asked for people to start shouting out ideas. Gary quickly stopped me and asked, "First, why are we doing this?" "Doing what?" I replied. "This brainstorming session," he said. I answered, "Duh! Because we want more students." He said, "But *really* why? Do you want more of the same kind of students or a broader variety of people? Do you want more students because you want to expand the image of the organization within the market place or to grow revenue? One might lead to the other, but you have to know the *why* before you can plan the *how*." I hate it when Gary is right.

The *one reason we exist* is not determined by the brainstorming team; that is like asking everyone sitting in the coach section on an airplane to decide the destination of the flight. Company leaders hash this question out long before the team meets. They also decide on Step One…

Step One-Ultimate Goal

Before gathering your brainstorming team, you must first decide the *ultimate goal; w*hat do you want when the entire process is finished? This step focuses on the eventual outcome. For our brainstorming for the *School of Improv*, we determined the Ultimate Goal was to double the number of students within twelve months. For the printing company I spoke of at the beginning of the book, the Ultimate Goal was:

1) Develop dozens of usable ideas.

2) Have twelve of those ideas put in "the vault" for later consideration.

3) Two ideas would need to be such that they could be implemented immediately.

4) Each of the two ideas would need to generate $1 million in revenue annually.

It might seem counter to the creative process to plan such a specific outcome, but without a date, number, and dollar amount attached to the goal, you won't get the results you need to grow your organization. And of course, the Ultimate Goal should serve the *one reason* you exist. The Ultimate Goal needs to be something you can measure and track. A goal of "A more positive company image for the public" may illuminate a problem, but it is an unworkable goal. It is not a measurable, track-able outcome.

You may be able to measure public perception after the completion of a PR project and discover that it is forty five percent higher than before the initiative, but you wouldn't know how you got there. It is impossible to track "better." Think in terms of what you can measure along the way. Then you can better evaluate initiatives and decide which to keep and which aren't working.

Step Two-Immediate Objectives

When I finally answered Gary's questions during the *School of Improv* brainstorming session, I was anxious to get things started. Just as I was preparing to gather ideas, he stopped me again and said, "Wait. How long are we meeting today?" I answered impatiently, "Three hours." He continued, "You don't expect us to achieve the entire goal today do you?" "No," I replied. He replied, "Then let's figure out exactly what we can accomplish in the three hours we have."

An unclear process can cause stress. In fact, studies have shown that one of the greatest stress factors for humans is uncertainty. Remember earlier when I mentioned that the brain actually values security over freedom? The same studies discovered that brain can adjust to accept almost any living condition as *normal*. Once the brain resets itself to the new expectations, what used to cause stress is no longer stressful. For instance, you love your beautiful house, nice car, and satisfying job. The thought of losing them would cause a great deal of stress. If you suddenly did lose your job, your house, and car, you would feel terrible at first. However, eventually your brain would reset its expectations to accept your new situation as normal. Eventually, not having those nice things will no longer be stressful.

As long as life is predictable—whether luxurious or full of hardship—stress is kept at bay. Surprisingly, the one condition the brain cannot adjust to is a daily commute to work. If your commute is a leisurely drive through the country, you actually lower stress levels. However, if there is any amount of traffic en route, that highly unpredictable situation causes stress; no matter how often you drive the route. Removing unpredictability in the brainstorm process can help enhance creativity.

Determining the Ultimate Goal will clear up debates about overall direction. Having Immediate Objectives improves focus by letting everyone know exactly what you expect during the next few hours. At the printing company brainstorming meeting, Gary and I told the group what we expected for each two-hour segment; that way the group could stay focused. People actually worry less about what is going to happen next if you tell them exactly what that *next* is. We helped the printing executives maintain focus by also letting them know what would happen with the *results* of each phase. There is nothing worse than putting in good effort without knowing what will become of your work. Before you start any meeting during the eight-step process, let the group know exactly what you expect to accomplish by the end of the meeting as well as how you will communicate with them about the results.

Another company I worked with was having an initial meeting to introduce three new directors of the department. When each director finished laying out their strategies for the coming year, they opened the meeting to questions from the team. One staff member asked, "How will we know if we disappoint you?" This was a very good question to ask at this stage of the getting-to-know-you process.

Knowing the Ultimate Goal and Immediate Objectives is good, but it also helps to let the group know how you will communicate with them and how they will be evaluated. When the directors answered the question above, they each reported a different way of communicating disappointment. One said that when he gets angry he usually shuts down. "If you see me retreat to my office," he said, "that is a sign I am not happy. It might seem childish, but that is how I handle stress. It keeps me from going off on an employee." Another director said she was raised in a family that had an in-your-face environment. She said that if she got angry, she would go directly to the source to talk things out. The third director said she was pretty easy going so she so rarely got angry unless someone flat-out dropped the ball. In such cases, she preferred to have a quiet and respectful conversation in a neutral environment like the cafeteria or break room. She didn't like having tough conversations in her office because the environment felt too authoritative.

As I said before, having too large of a group take part in the Foundation Phase (determining the Ultimate Goal and Immediate Objectives) is unproductive. Folks are just fine having this stuff figured out before they are invited to participate. Now that the first two steps are covered, you can move on to the rest. This is where the real brainstorming begins.

CHAPTER 5

Idea Generation

This is the part of the process that most people are familiar with, the actual *brainstorming* phase. However, there is one more step before the ideas start flying. You have already identified the single most important reason your organization exists; now it is time to do some *assumption checking*. This is where you look at who you are and what you do and separate fact from fiction.

Before brainstorming customer service ideas for a large retail company, I met with a group of 40 team leads and managers. "Pull out a piece of paper," I told them, "and write down all the adjectives you would use to describe someone who works here." They responded with words like *energetic, committed, approachable,* and *friendly.* I explained, "You can't develop new ideas unless you know your identity. Although it is vital to know what you are trying to get done, first you have to know who you are. Every organization has a culture, and the ideas we generate must support that culture.

I continued. "But, you have to be sure the words you use to identify your culture are shared by your customers. Now write down all the adjectives your customer might use to describe you." I paused and added, "And, be honest." And honest they were. The adjectives they felt would most likely used by their customers were *distant, unhappy,* and *clock-punchers*. Actually, you have to admire this group's ability to set aside their ego when assessing themselves. This exercise sure clarified what work had to be done.

When we conducted the brainstorming session for the *School of Improv,* we did the same exercise. We asked the group to list adjectives to describe what kind of person would take a class in improvisation. The responses were very much influenced by whether the adjective came from a current student, a former student, or someone unfamiliar to us. The current students used words like *creative, free-thinking,* and *open minded*. The former students (the ones who likely left because their needs weren't met by the class) wrote *distant, unwelcoming,* and *cliquey*. We thought that those unfamiliar with improv would at least assume that it was a creative and exciting process. Their adjectives were *weird, aloof,* and *stand-offish*.

Although these insights did not, in and of themselves, offer ideas to reach the goal, you can't start generating ideas until you have taken a good look at your organization. You must separate assumption from reality. Even though we thought of ourselves as open minded, the public thought of us as stand-offish. In the brief time we had with the invited guests at our brainstorming session, we were able to demonstrate that we were anything but aloof. How could we educate the rest of the public? Achieving a more accurate and positive public image was not one of our original goals. Even though this exercise did not change our goal of doubling the size of the school, it was necessary for us to clarify our image before we could move on.

The assumptions you discuss should include *who we are, what we sell, who we sell to, who we sell against*; and every aspect of your company. Once these are on the table, you will have a better idea of the obstacles you might face in reaching your Ultimate Goal.

In 2006, a team of six business executives from the Center for Association Leadership and the American Society for Association Executives in Washington, DC co-authored and published *Seven Measures of Success: What Remarkable Associations Do That Others Don't*. Using the same methodology that inspired the best-sellers *Built to Last* and *Good to Great*, the authors set out to determine the differences between highly successful non-profit associations and associations that simply survived from year to year.

Take, for instance, organizations that serve senior citizens. There are hundreds of senior-oriented non-profit organizations in the United States, but the American Association for Retired Persons, AARP, is the largest of them all. What does AARP do that others don't? I recommend reading *Seven Measures of Success* even if your organization is not a non-profit. Good business leaders know that business is business, and every industry has something to teach every other industry. When Pamela and I first opened *Stevie Ray's,* we were new business owners eager to learn from any source possible. We attended every workshop and seminar we could, no matter who conducted it. One workshop featured the owner of several restaurants in the Denver area. We didn't own a restaurant, but went anyway. We picked up an incredible amount of useful tidbits that easily crossed over from restaurant to improv company.

One of the differences discussed in *The Seven Measures of Success* is that successful organizations are data-driven, whereas average companies are assumption-driven. It is amazing how many organizations make colossal decisions based on nothing more than *this seems to make sense.* Since AARP is a membership organization, their mission is to serve the members. Rather than simply assume what the members want, AARP does something outlandish, it asks the members what they want. AARP members are surveyed constantly; and the philosophy within the organization is to never question the responses. The organization simply does what the member survey says to do. This results in AARP having some of the highest member satisfaction and retention ratings in the business.

We discovered this in our own company. I often give away free tickets to our comedy shows at corporate workshops.

One night I was talking to my wife about my company wanting to gain more accurate feedback about our ticket prices and show content. She suggested that, in order for recipients to receive the free tickets I offer, they should first have to complete a short survey. The survey could ask about what they might expect to pay when attending a comedy show, how far they would be willing to drive, and what kind of content they would be comfortable viewing.

We instituted the survey and immediately gained valuable feedback. We learned that our pricing was appropriate, which helped us avoid a costly change in ticket prices. We had always prided ourselves on offering comedy that was inoffensive. Our assumption was solidified by the feedback from the survey, which helped us market clean comedy more vigorously. And we learned that people assumed our location was farther away from the metro area than it actually is, which helped us redesign our website and make our location more attractive. The best part is, the survey is a low-cost online service that takes almost no effort to manage. I love telling people it was my idea (I hope my wife doesn't read this book).

It is easy for a company to dismiss client feedback with an attitude of *we know best*. Negative comments can be explained away with "they don't know the inner workings of the company" or "the bad situation they describe is highly unusual." Running an organization based on assumptions is dangerous, but a lot easier on the ego. At one company I worked with, I asked the upper management why they never surveyed their customers. They replied, "Because we're afraid of what we will hear." If you construct your brainstorm team correctly, you have willing participants in a room ready to tell you all about your company; from every perspective. Don't waste it. Ask the outsiders for their unfettered opinions about your company. Get former employees or customers who will be honest about their experiences.

Step Three-Idea Generation

It is finally time to get some ideas on paper, so let's talk about the paper itself. Well, not the paper really, but how you use it. One reason it is hard to get the right amount of energy going in a brainstorming session is the ideas come too slowly. This is because of the scribe, the person writing down the ideas. Just how the scribe records the ideas will affect the process.

First, don't have just one scribe. It is impossible to build energy when you have to wait for one person to write down the idea. Someone calls out a really cool idea and you want to tag onto it and add something, but you hear, "Wait. Let me finish writing down what Bob said." With the speed at which ideas enter your head, having to wait can cause many of them to drift away before being recorded. Have one scribe for every 5-10 people in the room. The process is simple; when one person calls out an idea, Scribe A repeats the idea loudly. This is Scribe A signaling to the other scribes *I've got this one*. When the next person calls out an idea, Scribe B repeats it loudly and writes it down. If the ideas are coming as fast as they should, usually Scribe A is still writing down the first idea. This makes the process smooth, but also keeps the energy up. Also, don't stick with one set of scribes throughout the Idea Generation step. Change writers every so often. This not only gives the scribes a break, but you also don't lose all the good ideas the scribes themselves might offer. Seeing all the different styles of handwriting also adds a bit of variety to the process.

The next rule is important; *no paraphrasing*. It always happens that, when someone calls out an idea, either the scribe or someone in the group will paraphrase the idea in simpler terms. When a member of the group explains an idea for reaching new demographics, someone else cuts them of with, "Oh, you mean expand our marketing." This simple act seems harmless, but it has devastating effects on brainstorming.

First, if *expand our marketing* is what they meant to say, they would have said it. Second, by paraphrasing an idea, you miss the subtle meaning that goes with it. Paraphrasing dumbs an idea down to its basic element. This might seem reasonable because it gets to the root of the idea, but the root isn't what you are after. The *root* of an idea about marketing is what makes it the same as every other marketing idea. You don't want the root, you want the fruit; the intricate details that make the idea *unlike* what you have done before.

To get the fruit, every idea must be written down verbatim; no changes or edits. Another reason this rule is important is because it results in more participation from the group. When you paraphrase someone else's idea, you also short-circuit their brain. Before you paraphrased for them, their brain was zipping around thinking up cool stuff. When you paraphrase for someone else, you are doing their thinking for them; so they stop thinking. They usually say to themselves, "That's not what I meant, but okay." After this brief glitch, they have a difficult time getting back into the creative flow. You will find that the person will not speak for a while. They aren't necessarily afraid that someone will re-phrase their thoughts again, their brains have just been short-circuited and they need time to reboot. The simple—and seemingly harmless—act of paraphrasing has essentially removed a member of your team. To avoid this, when the scribes repeat ideas called out, they must repeat them exactly as they were said and write them down verbatim.

The speed of this process shouldn't be short-changed. This is one place where Osborne, the inventor of the brainstorm process, got it right. You want a high volume of ideas; quantity begets quality. Companies involved in product development will tell you that it takes 1,000-3,000 ideas for one to make it to production. Think back to the last brainstorming session you attended. How many ideas were generated? Usually twenty five or so; a bit short of the thousands needed.

Get a few pads of poster paper; the kind where you can tear the pages off the pad and stick them to the wall. As soon as one page is filled with dozens of ideas, tear it off the pad and stick it to the wall. Pretty soon the room will be filled with crazy ideas. Try to avoid an Idea Generation session where one or two people have small pads of paper sitting in front of them. Whatever ideas they write down might as well disappear because no one else in the group can see them. This also causes a drop in energy. While everyone suggests ideas, the scribe writes them down. After a while, someone asks, "How many ideas do we have so far?" The scribe silently adds them up and says, "Fourteen." After a pause, the group starts calling out more ideas.

After a short period of adding ideas, someone usually asks, "Are any of the ideas we have so far any good?" This is not an attempt to find the best solution; it is a way of ending the torturous meeting. Being able to look around the room and see all the ideas in front of you makes it easier to generate even more. As each page is torn from the pad and stuck on the wall, the room begins to fill with ideas; the group gains more energy just seeing what they have accomplished so far. As you look at the list, your brain makes new connections between the existing ideas. As the pages fill up the room, the group will see how many more they can create, competing with themselves to do better. You can achieve that with one person sitting at a legal pad waiting for the group to wake up.

Remember when I discussed how children say *yes* to themselves by offering their ideas with excitement and enthusiasm? Don't allow people to offer suggestions meekly. If someone starts with, "I'm not sure about this, but..." stop them. Remind them that the manner in which they call out their idea will greatly affect how others participate. The rule must be that everyone calls out their idea as if it is the best idea ever. This may seem like you are playing the part of the over-excited cheerleader, but *how* an idea is offered is just as important as *what* the idea is.

Just as children say *yes* to their partners, it is important to monitor the ideas are received. When the scribes repeat an idea, they must match the positive energy of the group. Simply adding a little volume and liveliness to how the scribes call-back an idea will yield better results from the team.

This is your brain on brainstorming

It is easy to get discouraged when the first dozen or so ideas sound old and familiar. That is the way the brain works. Now is when the dance between the right and left hemispheres of the brain begins. The left hemisphere is responsible for immediate associations while the right hemisphere works on a whole-picture level. While problem solving, the brain engages the left hemisphere first; hoping to find the answer as quickly as possible. If the answer lies with a quick association, (i.e. what worked in the past might work again) the brain gets to solve the problem with minimal effort. This pattern in the brain causes all brainstorming to start with simple, easily understood, and recognizable ideas.

It is only after the left hemisphere has exhausted all its immediate association that the right brain takes over. In fact, an individual will most likely reach a point of frustration before developing a great idea. This is a sign that the left brain has churned through every obvious association it can make. Not having any success, it relinquished the task to the other hemisphere. The process of burning through all the easy ideas is hard work. It takes a lot of energy; and coming up empty handed is frustrating. You finally hit a point where the brain says, "Fine. If you don't like any of these ideas, take over right hemisphere!" Basically, creativity is hard work and the part of the brain that is capable of creating the ideas you want has to be forced to participate (only after the left side is forced to relinquish control). Sounds like me and my wife, Kanitta, when it comes to relinquishing control of the car. It only happens when the other person is completely exhausted.

Once all the tried-and true ideas are on the table, the right brain gets its turn; and broader, big-picture ideas emerge. Don't despair at the beginning of the Idea Generation step.

If the group gets frustrated, assure them that great ideas are right around the corner, as long as they continue to work. Note, however, there is a difference between staying focused on the process and hitting a stress wall. If frustration gets too high, the brain will shut down.

I am brain dead

Hitting a dead spot is one of the most difficult challenges in the Idea Generation step. When you look around a room and see everyone's energy gone and they obviously just want to out of there, it can be difficult to know what to do. Most well-meaning facilitators say, "Come on everyone, let's focus." Asking a person who has lost all energy to focus is like asking a person in a wheelchair to run a race. The desire is there, but the tools are not.

Low energy spots are a perfect time to use a whole-brain game. Brain-dead moments call for a quick release of stress, some laughter; a quick diversion so alpha waves can be generated and ideas can flow again. The group, wanting a strong leader, will be grateful to have someone acknowledge what everyone already knows, that the energy is gone. The facilitator should state frankly, "It looks like we've hit a wall. Everyone up and let's play a whole-brain game." All it takes is a few minutes of play to recharge the room. Don't try to force the game to relate to the subject of the brainstorming; clearing everyone's head is the goal.

Another way to trick the brain into creativity is to access its most efficient function; pattern recognition. The easiest thing for the brain to do is find patterns in our environment and fall into them. To the brain, patterns equal familiarity and productivity. To use this to your advantage, try a technique I call *Random Word*. I was conducting a brainstorm session with a large group of arts organizations. They wanted to create a new arts district in their area. During the Idea Generation step, we had gone through all the obvious ideas and the group had reached an impasse. The energy was beginning to wane, so I told the group that each person would be given a word at random. The word would have nothing to do with the arts or the goal at hand. Once each person was given their word, they would use the word to create new ideas. Most often, simple word association creates ideas.

I gave people in the group words like *cheese, travel,* and *pets*. Then I told them to play some internal word association and see what came up. Word association (saying the first word that comes to mind) accesses the pattern function of the brain, so ideas come easily; without thought or planning. Playing solo word association is difficult because the brain can get stuck in a pattern—*horse, saddle, rider,* etc. In improvisation we have a game called *Word Ball*, which is a group version of word association. When word association is played in groups, a wider variety of words is generated. In a group each word is more easily disconnected from previous words. This is because a person thinking alone will follow a pattern. Patterned thinking is the easiest function of the brain, so we usually think in straight lines. In a group, people create different patterns because everyone's brain is moving in different directions. Simply by virtue of working with others, your brain is forced out of its own patterned thinking.

In Word Ball, you pass words randomly around a circle, saying the first word that connects to the one given to you. It is best if you forget all the words said previous to the one thrown to you. This might result in *horse, saddle, weight, train, pet*, etc. When *saddle* is taken with no connection to *horse*, its meaning can be to "saddle" someone with responsibility, so the next word might be *weight*. *Weight* sounds like *wait*, which could make the next person think of waiting for a *train*, which makes the next person think of training a *pet*.

Word Ball is an easy game to clear the mind; especially because no one is allowed to question someone else's word. The rule of *Trust* is enhanced because judgment is withheld. You might also be surprised at how much laughter occurs during a simple game like Word Ball. There are only a few basic causes of laughter. The Laws of Laughter below are more fully explained in *What We Laugh At...and Why* by the world-renowned author Stevie Ray.

> 1) Laughter of Recognition. We laugh when someone relates an experience similar to one we have experienced.

2) Laughter of Superiority. Most laughter is the result of someone acting like a fool and our resulting feeling of superiority.

3) Laughter of the Unexpected. Most surprises, unless they are scary, result in laughter.

4) Laughter of Delight. In the right environment, people laugh simply because they are gathered in a group. They celebrate the delightful union of people by laughing together.

The unexpected responses in Word Ball cause surprise and laughter.

During the Random Word game for the arts professionals, the man who got *travel* played Word Ball with himself. I heard him say, *travel, road, freedom, motorcycle*. All of a sudden he shouted, "How about we organize a motorcycle art crawl?" The entire room said, "Cool! That has never been done before. What a great way to get middle-aged people out to see arts stuff in a fun, outdoor activity. Rather than the usual motorcycle rally that goes from bar to bar, they can go from a gallery to a short theatre performance, to a dance recital, to whatever." A market-disruptive idea is one that entirely changes how a service or product is offered. It may change how the market even perceived the product. It is the kind of idea that drives the competition to say, "Why didn't we think of that?" The motorcycle art crawl became a whole new way of marketing and delivering an old product; and it all came from one random word.

No negating

I have already discussed why healthy debate and criticism enhance the brainstorming process, and there is time built later into the process for that; but not right now. Now is for a high volume of ideas. The best way to get there is not to spend too much time debating one idea. This is where the *"yes, and"* rule of improvisation comes in handy.

When someone calls out an idea, someone else should *"yes, and"* it. This does not mean everyone actually likes the idea or thinks it will work; in fact, people may come back later and argue against it. The point is to use the *"yes, and"* rule to generate a high volume of ideas

"Let's have free doughnuts in the break room"

"*Yes, and* let's tie the type of doughnut each week into the current project of the department."

"*Yes, and* we can create slogans for each week, with departments competing for the best slogan."

It is very easy at this stage to get bogged down discussing the worth of each idea. The facilitator's job is to prevent a blockage of ideas. Debate will come later. At this stage, the *Eight Rules of Improv* are a good guideline for keeping the process productive (page 31).

We tried that once already

The phrase, "We tried that once already." is one of the most common comments heard during brainstorming. "We tried that once already." must be banned; from business, from the home, from all human communication. (Am I being a bit extreme?) The reason "We already tried that idea and it didn't work." is a useless statement is that it never provides an idea; it only kills the one offered by someone else.

Sure, some ideas have been tried and they failed, but past failures are irrelevant because *timing is everything*. Even a year or two can make the difference between success and failure for the same concept. When the idea was last tried, the context might have been different. One small element of the plan could change to turn disaster into triumph. Replace this worthless phrase with, "The last time we tried that it didn't work. Let's talk about why." This leads to discussion, which leads to new ideas. Discussion about why a failure occurred helps flush out current ideas.

"We tried that once already." only comes from *experts* who think they have the experience to keep the rest of the group from making a grave mistake. Trusting experts is not always a good idea. Consider that the CEO of 3M ordered Dick Drew to stop working on the research that led to the invention of masking tape and scotch tape. The *expert* knew that Drew was wasting his time. After all, Drew was not a scientist, he was a salesman. Had Drew listened to the expert, one of the most profitable and useful products we use today would never have been invented.

Sylvester Stallone spent years trying to get motion picture companies to produce a new movie that he had written, *Rocky*. Every movie executive that was interested in the project said they would produce the movie, but they couldn't see him playing the lead role. They were sure that Stallone, a largely unknown actor, could not pull off the role of a meat-and-potatoes boxer taking on the world champion. The movie executives were very stubborn. They even offered Stallone tidy sums of money to sell the movie rights *without* him acting the main role. After all, when it came to movies, *they* were the experts. Stallone stuck to his convictions, and the rest is movie pugilism history. Experts, if they knew half as much as they thought they knew, they would know twice as much as they actually know. You know?

Are you kidding?

Some ideas just can't be taken seriously. Or can they? The Idea Generation step is one in which everyone must turn off the brain's censor, the right prefrontal cortex, and allow crazy to happen. The reason it takes 1,000-3,000 ideas for one to be successful is because the best, most creative, most market-disruptive ideas are generated after people get past the sensible ones. Crazy often equals profit. Inhibiting the goofiness of the process is counterproductive.

Historically, the most profitable ideas were met with the most resistance. Since the brain reacts poorly to change, it stands to reason that an out-there idea would get a lot of push-back from others, at least at first. Lucky for us consumers, for every great product we love, there was someone who championed the idea; saying no to everyone who said no. Otherwise, the world would not have had Earth Shoes, Spray-On Hair, and the Thigh Master.

In *Imagine*, Jonah Lehrer discusses a concept called *conceptual blending*. Conceptual blending is when the brain skips around its tendency to file information in appropriate categories and instead connects ideas that don't belong together. This happens when old solutions are tied to new situations, or when seemingly silly ideas are discovered to have profound truths. Conceptual blending can be engaged by giving someone an impossible riddle and then telling them a seemingly unrelated story. Within the story lies the answer to the problem; conceptual blending connects the two.

Because of the power of conceptual blending, facilitators must not tolerate foolish ideas, they must encourage them. This is not possible if the group is focused on an outcome that appears immediately workable. The printing company CEO I spoke of at the beginning of this book had difficulty leading his brainstorming session because he was worried about saving the company from impending doom. He immediately evaluated each suggestion as to whether it was a company-saving idea. He used his *expertise* to evaluate each suggestion and ended up destroying some of the best ideas.

One of my passions is martial arts. I have trained in several styles since starting in 1977 and currently hold four black belts. When a person born in the U.S. hears that I have trained in several disciplines, they are usually impressed. They consider my approach to have balance because I have broad-based experience. However, when someone from an Asian country hears about my varied training, they are suspicious. They consider my approach to *lack* balance because I did not focus my efforts; choosing instead to scatter my attention.

My first karate instructor, Kiyohisa Okamura, was a Japanese master of Goju-Ryu karate and Judo. Goju-Ryu is the style featured in the original version of the movie, *The Karate Kid*. Mr. Okamura told me that jumping from style to style was frowned upon in old-school martial arts circles. "We call it 'dojo hopping,'" he said. (*Dojo* is Japanese for "place of the way," and is used to refer to any martial arts training studio.) He told me the classic Asian philosophy for attaining mastery, *He who chases two rabbits gets no dinner.*

Okamura explained the martial arts training philosophy to his students by holding out a fist. Pointing to his fist, he said, "This is your art. This is what you hope to achieve. What is preventing you from reaching you art is a big shell." He made a large circling motion around the fist. "In order to reach your art you must chip away at the shell. Every day you train, you chip a little bit more of the shell until one day you finally reach your art hidden inside. When that day comes, you will no longer need me. I tell you to leave or stay, but you have learned all you can from me.

"The only way to reach your art is to listen to your sensei (teacher). A good master can guide you to your art because we know what it looks like, we've been there before. Do not follow someone who is only one step ahead of you or has read perhaps one more book than you. They may be able to teach you a few things, but they cannot help you attain mastery because they have not reached their art. They don't know how to make each step count."

"If you train without a good teacher, or with a bad teacher, your chipping at the shell every day may take you around and around; not each step toward the center. You might accidentally find your art; you may never find it. Following a good teacher is important because we can make sure that every step you take is toward your goal."

These are wise words indeed, but also influenced by culture. The advice certainly has worth, but look at its impact on the whole. In older Asian communities, creativity is not as highly respected as adherence to tradition. When Okamura took me to visit other karate masters in Japan, I was shown a fine piano in the home of some friends. The family asked if I played piano and I told them I was not trained, but played by ear. They asked me to play and I improvised some music. They nodded politely and asked, "Do you play any real songs?"

My hosts were not trying to be impolite; it is just that they valued tradition over improvisation. The martial arts are known for being bound by tradition, which is the perfect atmosphere to develop a respect for rituals and history. However, if a martial arts technique is discovered to be less than perfect it can difficult to get that time-honored technique removed from the training manual of an old-school studio.

Here is another example of how culture can affect creativity. There is a fairly well-known poster of a lone fish swimming in front of an entire school. During a study on cultural attitudes, people in western countries were shown the poster and asked to describe the solitary fish. They used words like *leader, self-directed,* and *confident.* People in the west are taught that striking out from the pack and forging your own path is to be admired. However, when people in eastern countries were asked to interpret the same image they used words like *antisocial, uncooperative, and rule breaker.* The predominant opinion in eastern countries was that the lone fish was not a team player and unable to fit into society. In the east, working together toward a common goal is more important than personal achievement. This is why many Asian and eastern

European countries place one's last name (the family name) first. My karate instructor would introduce himself as Okamura, Kiyohisa to demonstrate that his lineage is more important than his individual self.

The eastern philosophy that individuality is considered damaging has many traditional martial arts studios following the philosophy of *hammer the nail into place.* Okamura explained that, when you practice karate on a wooden floor in bare feet, stepping on a nail that had popped up would be painful. A student—or employee, family member, etc.—who attempted to stand out from the group was also considered a nail who had popped up. Their need for individuality was considered just as damaging to the dojo as a nail popping up from the floor. The teacher's job was to pound the nail flat by making the student realize that the group was more important than the individual, thereby returning order to the dojo.

This philosophy is also practiced in the American military. Much of military basic training involves teaching each soldier to think of his or her unit before self. While watching a training video for the Navy SEALS, I saw the drill instructor admonish a recruit by saying, "Why don't you just drop out, boy? You consider yourself an individual! You are no good to a team if you're an individual." Simply calling a recruit an *individual* was considered an insult.

The world would be a better place if we all thought a bit more about the needs of others before our own, but this philosophy breeds efficiency and teamwork. It does not breed innovation. Anyone who has trained in a classic martial art will tell you that the very spirit of the training lives in the fact that nothing has changed for thousands of years. This is wonderful for respecting tradition, but not for enhancing creativity.

Mastery has its place, but in brainstorming no one can profess to know what the art looks like at the end of the road. No one has been there to see. A facilitator must not only expect creativity and innovation, but he or she must be prepared to accept the challenges that come with such an atmosphere. The process can feel chaotic and the participants are not as controlled as in standard work environments. In fact, the very people you need in order to instill creativity may be the hardest to work with.

In *Imagine*, Jonah Lehrer cites a study conducted by Skidmore College in which several dozen elementary school teachers were asked whether they wanted creative kids in their classroom. Every teacher said yes. The same teachers were asked to rate their students on a variety of personality measures. The traits most closely aligned with creative thinking (free expression, for instance), were related to the teachers' least favorite students. Basically, the teachers all said they wanted creative kids in the classroom, but hated creative behavior. Free thinkers tend to be harder to control and do poorly on standardized tests. These types of students are admonished in classrooms and do not advance in workplaces where employees' actions are tightly controlled.

After reading this far in the book, you can probably imagine what I was like as a student. Throughout my school years, teachers routinely put "extremely social" in the comment section of my evaluations. Imagine if they had been able to use the term "pain in the ass" instead. I was lousy at tests because strict structure drove me crazy. (And yet, I totally dig the structure and traditions of martial arts, and excelled in the highly structured world of the Boy Scouts. Go figure.)

While attending junior high school, the history department wanted to try an experiment. They developed a project meant to develop our abilities at setting and achieving long-term goals. The students of two history classes were combined and we were told to form working teams. The students were allowed to choose their own members. Each team would develop a project concerning history. The teams would brainstorm ideas for their project, submit their choice to the teacher, and the teacher would select the project for the team. Throughout the entire semester, half of each class day would be devoted to standard history teaching. During the second half of class the teams would gather to work on their projects. Half of every student's grade would depend on the group project.

It was almost the end of the semester when, during the second half of a history class, my teacher noticed that I wasn't sitting with a team. "Steve, why aren't you with your group?" he asked. "Huh?" I replied. "Which group are you with?" he asked. "What group?" I replied. "The group for the semester project." he said. "What project?" I asked. During the explanation of the project at the beginning of the semester, I just happened to be distracted and didn't hear him. After that, whenever the groups gathered to work on their projects, I just busied myself with more important work. (The subject of which escapes me now, but you can be assured that it was valuable stuff.) You can imagine the conversation that took place between the school and my parents.

Leaving aside for a moment whether a teacher should have noticed that one student was sitting alone every day during group time, especially for an entire semester; the point of the story is he wanted to fail me and hold me back a grade. My parents were a bit wiser about the situation. They said, "If Steve isn't interested in something, you can't *make* him interested in it. He is not that kind of learner. Tests aren't even an accurate way to measure his learning. We just know that, when he finds what he truly wants to do, he will excel at that." That, of course, was not what they told me when they got home after the parent teacher conference.

Lo and behold, my parents were right. I was able to graduate high school, create my own degree in college, build a company from scratch, and just recently, I even learned to dress myself (my wife's opinion notwithstanding). This is not an indictment of the education process, but a reminder that those who are the most difficult to *manage* may be the very people who will give you the very ideas you need.

Don't try to force creativity or it will elude you altogether. Keith Johnstone says in *Impro*, "Ask people to give you an original idea and see the chaos it throws them into. If they said the first thing that came into their head, there'd be no problem." He says of trying to be original, "It is like a man at the North Pole trying to walk north... Striving after originality takes you far away from your true self, and makes your work mediocre."

> *Acting is behaving truthfully*
> *under imaginary circumstances.*
> Sanford Meisner

The quote above is from one of the most important figures in the history of theatre. Meisner developed a style of acting called "The Method" which has been used to train some of the foremost actors of our day. Meisner's quote was illustrated during an exercise I used while working with a group of MBA professors. I was hired to help the professors shift from lecture-based teaching to the more effective method of interactive learning. At one point during the workshop, I had them form three-person teams. Each person was to present a learning objective to their teammates. Each group would devise interactive exercises that would teach the lesson.

While walking around the room, one group looked stumped. When I asked what the problem was, one professor said, "I want my students to learn to create business plans. Currently, I have them invent a new business and create a business plan accordingly. I don't allow them to use existing businesses. The problem is they can never come up with ideas for a brand new business."

I laughed and said, "If inventing a new business was that easy, everyone would be business owners. Try this instead, have three students volunteer to act the part of a 'family.' Have the rest of the class watch as the family stands in one corner of the room. Each of them—mother, father, and child—gets ready for their day. They move from the corner of the classroom a few feet to 'the kitchen' where they have breakfast. They continue around the room, each going through a different part of their day. By the time they get all the way around the room they are having dinner and getting ready for bed. As this goes on, the rest of the class observes and looks for elements of the family's day they can improve. That will lead to a new business idea." This proved to be a very effective brainstorming tool for his classes.

Role playing can feel silly or uncomfortable for some, but it is a valuable tool in creating useful ideas. For instance, if you are trying to develop a smoother customer-service process for your phone staff, have people play real-life scenarios. Have people play the part of a customer calling your company. People can either use real-life problems or invent new ones on the spot. This is much more effective than simply sitting around a table describing a typical interaction, because *living it*—seeing it played in front of you—sparks the imagination in ways that talking never can. One company I worked with had a very efficient process for shipping products to customers, but sometimes the drive for efficiency can leave the customer feeling left out. During the Idea Generation step, I had one of the company's staff members conduct a routine call to a customer to set up an order. I made sure to have the customer played by one of the outsiders invited to participate in the brainstorm session. Having a staff member play the part of the customer could lose the reality of the situation. The real reaction of the customer is where valuable ideas come from.

During the role-play, it was obvious what was missing. The process was smooth and efficient, but the customer was visibly frustrated. I say "visibly" because we were able to see the emotion during the brainstorming session in ways that were never possible during a routine phone call. The company executives were perplexed because they had various means of gaining customer feedback; phone surveys following calls, online questionnaires, etc. Even with all these channels of feedback, they never knew that this frustration existed. The role-play experience helped the company create an ongoing and more accurate means of tracking customer satisfaction. They no longer rely solely on opt-in surveys or online questionnaires. They review customer calls to discern any sign of frustration that might be missed by the sales professional.

Offering customers a chance to provide feedback is crucial. However, if people are angry or frustrated they will skip the survey; and skip doing business with you. The most accurate way to *know* the experience of the customer is to *live* it. Theatre directors are given the advice that—during the run of a production—they should watch the play from every seat in the theatre. Role-playing is a great way to sit in every seat that you ask your customer to occupy.

One last word about the Idea Generation step; numbers. When Gary and I were working with a group of executives and we were ready to start this step, we asked them how many ideas they thought they could create in two hours. The answers ranged from 50-100. "That's no good," Gary said. "If it takes almost three thousand ideas for one to work, we need a lot more than fifty. How about we shoot for one thousand ideas in two hours?" We waited until the group retrieved their jaws from the floor, at which time they said things that I can't repeat in polite company.

"Are you crazy? We can't come up with a thousand ideas!" they all cried. I jumped in with, "Okay, how many ideas do you think you *can* create?" They thought for a moment and said, "Maybe five hundred." We chuckled and said, "A moment ago your highest goal was fifty ideas. Now, after we suggested one thousand, your goal is ten times fifty." We continued, "It is very typical to take a goal and cut it in half. That way you feel sure you can reach it. What is in a number anyway? Why did you say fifty? Why did we say one thousand? You said fifty because you didn't want to fail. We said one thousand because we knew that having that many ideas was the only way to achieve the ultimate goal."

After some more discussion, we agreed to set the goal at five hundred ideas in two hours. We assured the group that the goal was easily attainable because we were not looking for five hundred *good* ideas; just five hundred thoughts written down. Lifting the burden of *usability* for each suggestion is crucial. At the end of two hours, we had 498 ideas. We fell short of the goal by two ideas, but everyone felt fantastic anyway. Part of the Immediate Objectives step is to decide exactly how many suggestions will be written down in the time you have allotted. Don't wimp out on the goal!

By the end of the Idea Generation step, you should have several poster-sized pages stuck on the walls around the room. If you have managed the energy of the room properly, the ideas should have flowed so fast that the scribes had difficulty keeping up (if so, use more scribes). Sloppy handwriting is a good sign of productivity. Take a step back and admire your work. Very few people take time to celebrate before moving on to the next project, give yourselves time to take in the creative ideas you have generated.

Step Four-Incubation

It is time for a break. Of all the steps in brainstorming, this is probably the one of which people are least aware. This step is enveloped in the phrase, "Let's sleep on it." The brain has a wonderful capacity to figure things out for us, but we refuse to get out of the way. Our conscious efforts certainly bear fruit. In fact, research shows that creativity is greatly enhanced by hard work and concerted effort. In short, creativity is hard work. Let's not forget, however, how much can be accomplished by stepping away from the task and taking a breather.

The Incubation Step should be long enough to let the subconscious work; overnight if possible. During this time, do not force yourself to think about the project. During incubation, disparate ideas will blend together to create new solutions. Alpha waves are generated during relaxing activities and "Ah ha" ideas pop up. Practitioners of meditation are taught not to block out thoughts, but to let them bump around freely in the mind. Rather than let a single thought dominate, you view it and let it move on.

Soon, the brain starts to create connections not possible with conscious attention. Ridding one's self of focus actually enhances it.

Jonah Lehrer cites a study in *Imagine* in which two neurologists, Ullrich Wagner and Jan Born, tested the power of dreams to solve problems. Test subjects were given a problem to solve. The problem contained a solution with a shortcut that was only illuminated if the subject had an insight about the problem itself. On average, only 20 percent of the subjects could solve the problem. However, those allowed to fall into REM dream-sleep solved the problem 60 percent of the time.

If you are unable to allow for a 24 hour incubation period, at least break for lunch or take a long walk. Try to move to surroundings that are relaxing. Daydreaming allows parts of our brain to work together that normally function separately. Scientists, artists, and developers report that some of their greatest insights come when they step away from the problem and let their subconscious take over.

That's about it for the Incubation step. If you have been reading steadily up until now, take a break.

Step Five – Regeneration

If a high volume of ideas is what you are after, this is the step that will give it to you. Since the group is just returning from a rejuvenating period of incubation, it is best to let them quietly jot their ideas down on paper. Give everyone a marker and tell them to do two things:

1) Write their new ideas down on the empty poster paper you have ready and waiting

2) Create new ideas by either changing existing ideas or combining different ideas to create something new.

Creative thinking often involves pairing two seemingly disparate ideas. The group should think, "What if we took part of this idea and part of that one and combined them?" Also, encourage the group to fantasize. They should have an attitude of, "Wouldn't it be cool if?"

As I said before, necessity is not the mother of invention, wishing is. If you had asked travelers in the 1970's the best way to plan a trip, they would have pulled out a map and unfolded it in front of you. If you had asked that same group in the 1980's, they would have produced a printout of MapQuest or a similar computer map program.

If you had asked the travelers if they liked the method they used, they would have said the maps and printouts worked just fine. Few of them would have told you, "I need a device that sits on my dashboard that displays a moving image with arrows directing me to my destination." Since the introduction of commercial GPS in the 1990s (the military had it since the 1960s), unfolding a map seems archaic. If you ask people if what they have works well, they will usually say that the tools they have are fine. People don't usually think in terms of how something could be made better until someone else points out something better. Then they see what is missing, or slow, or inconvenient.

Voice-activation was invented to enable a hands-off process, but what led the way was an attitude of, "Wouldn't it be cool if you didn't have to enter information by hand and just speak it instead?" All the stuff you see in futuristic movies comes from, "Wouldn't it be cool if…" not "I think this would be necessary." Frankly, if you focused too much on necessity, you wouldn't get much higher on Maslow's Hierarchy of Needs than food and shelter. Most cool things that are invented are things that we really don't need, but later we convince ourselves that we can't live without them.

After people have had some time to regenerate ideas on their own, have them work in pairs so they can bounce ideas off each other. Don't move into small groups right away, too many brains can cloud the process. During certain stages of the process, it is better to have just one other person with whom you can discuss your ideas.

A portion of time should be spent with the group identifying ideas they think warrant special attention. This is where lively debate comes into play. Participants should be prepared to defend their ideas; this critical thinking process flushes out more possibilities. Lehrer described how Pixar's called this the *crit* session. Pixar executive, Bobby Podesta, warns not to allow the criticism to become personal. He says, "It could get really depressing if all we did was shoot each other down. And that's why, when we do engage in criticism, we try to make sure the criticism is mixed with a little something else; a new idea that allows us to immediately move on, to start focusing not on the mistake, but on how to fix it." At Pixar this is called *plussing*, and sounds very similar to the *"yes, and..."* rule of improvisation.

Whereas the Idea Generation step is focused solely on volume, the Regeneration Step not only adds ideas, but also examines the usability of each idea. Idea Generation avoids too much critical thinking, regeneration adds the "How could we actually use this in real life?" component. Since great concepts come from unlikely pairings, ask the group to mash together two ideas that would never be seen on the same planet. Just as great lawyers are trained to be capable of arguing both the plaintiff's and defense's case with equal fervor, so too should your group. Divide your group into pro and con and have them present arguments defending their point of view. Have a scribe capture the salient points, these may come in handy during the implementation phase; or may develop new ideas on their own.

The end of the Regeneration Step can be a double-edged sword. People often leave feeling energized, but they can be a bit disconnected from the process because—unless they are a part of the implementation team—they have no idea what is going to happen next. If they are truly engaged in the process, they will worry about the outcome of their favorite ideas. Ease their minds by telling them the next steps; that a smaller group will meet to determine which ideas are to be used immediately and which will be saved for later. Let them know how you will communicate with them. Don't just shove them out the door; thank them for their participation by keeping them informed. Those who joined the process from outside your organization especially need to know who they will hear from and how.

CHAPTER 6

Implementation

Now that you have all these great ideas spread around the room, what's next? First, get rid of everyone. Okay, most of them. Whereas the Idea Generation phase of the process is better with lots of people, the Implementation Phase is hindered by too large a group. Resist the urge to have everyone involved in the entire eight-step process. People often do this out of a misguided sense of fairness; not wanting to exclude anyone. They are trying to gain consensus, but consensus is a misguided belief.

For generations, it was thought that the only way to make sure a team put full effort into a plan was to make sure everyone was in agreement. This seemed the only way to be fair to all concerned. I remember as a teenager complaining to my parents about something not being fair. They said, "The fair is at the end of August; go ride the Tilt-a-Whirl. That's the only place you'll find fair." This isn't to say that seeking fairness in the workplace is not a worthy goal; it is just impossible because the very people you are trying to treat fairly can't completely decide on what is fair themselves.

Fair treatment doesn't mean everyone is treated exactly the same. People want to be treatment in a way that respects their unique situation. Asking everyone to help implement a plan is like cramming fifteen pilots into the flight deck and expecting the plane to fly straight. Heck, just think back to when you and four friends tried to decide where to go to lunch. Thirty minutes into the *pizza vs. burger* debate, someone in the group groaned, "Someone just decide!" The Implementation Phase needs a small group of decision makers who know what kind of resources and constraints are in place.

The most important part of this phase is to get moving. Groups can become frozen by perfection; they don't want to move on an idea until they are sure that absolutely every obstacle is accounted for. Remember, *done is better than perfect*. An idea is rarely perfect when it is rolled out the door, just think of all the new software programs that need constant updates. If software companies waited until every single bug was worked out of the system, we would all still be playing Pong. If you don't know what Pong is, send this book back and I'll refund your money. I don't want you reading this book. Don't worry about perfection, what-ever you invent won't be flawless anyway. It will be a springboard for improvements.

When moving to the smaller group, it is important not to forget everyone who participated along the way. Make sure they know exactly what became of their ideas. You certainly don't need to go down the entire list of hundreds of suggestions and detail each outcome; focus on the big ideas that people were excited about and let the participants know if the idea was scrapped, will be held for later, or is being considered for immediate use. People are reasonable enough to know that some of their ideas will be discarded. All they want to know is that their input was valuable.

Before you tackle the first step, let's discuss how each idea should be viewed. It is common at this phase for the more rigid minded team members to look at a really wacky idea and say, "Well, we can start by throwing that one out." This is a mistake. Remember that the most profitable ideas in history were initially dismissed, or even ridiculed. Today, it is common knowledge that simple hand washing is the best way to prevent the spread of disease. The man who first introduced the concept in the mid-1800s was a Hungarian physician, Ignaz Semmelweis.

Semmelweis participated in a study to determine why one clinic in Vienna experienced lower infant mortality rates than another clinic in the area. Semmelweis noticed that in one clinic, the doctors went from working with cadavers directly to the delivery room. The other clinic, with the lower infant mortality rate, had no autopsy room. Since germ theory had no yet been created, Semmelweis concluded that the doctors in the first clinic must be carrying "cadaverous particles" which were causing illness and death.

During the 1800s, medicine was still based on the "Four Humours" theory. The four elements of the body were yellow bile, black bile, blood, and phlegm (each was also associated with the elements of Fire, Air, Earth, and Water). If the four essential elements, or humours, were in balance, the patient thrived. If the humours were out of balance, illness resulted. Coincidentally, this theory was the basis of the practice of blood-letting. It was thought that many illnesses were the result of too much blood, throwing off the balance of humours. Either applying leeches or cutting a vein and draining blood was thought to restore balance. Today, the practice of blood-letting is kept alive by the Internal Revenue Service.

Semmelweis believed that washing off the cadaverous particles would solve the infant mortality problem. He conducted research to prove his theory and published his findings in medical journals. Because his theory flew in the face of established medical beliefs, and since no one could see these particles, he was ridiculed. He spent the rest of his life promoting hygiene, but his theories were not accepted until after his death. Think of Semmelweis the next time you hear someone say, "Of course it's true. Everybody knows it."

When reviewing the ideas for the Implementation Phase, you are not looking for ideas that make sense, you are trying to make sense out of every idea. When we conducted the brainstorming session for the *School of Improv*, had we not been focusing on making sense out of the silly, the ideas suggested could have easily been tossed in the trash. I started the session by letting everyone know that the goal was to double the size of the school in twelve months. One of improv students called out, "Have everyone gain twice as much weight; that will double the size of the school." This is when some people would say, "Come on. Let's get serious." Rather than poo-poo the idea, we immediately repeated his idea out loud and wrote on the big board "Have everyone gain twice as much weight" (remember to write down every idea exactly as it is stated.) The next idea was, "Clone every existing student." That idea was repeated and written down. Next came, "Invite people from the island of Malta."

You can imagine how the rest of the day went. Later, when it came time for the committee to select which ideas to implement, it would have been easy to dismiss these first loony suggestions. Instead, it was our job to find the truth within the weirdness. When we looked at "Have everyone gain twice as much weight", we tried to discern what it really meant. Pamela Mayne, our Artistic Director, said, "You know, we used to ask the students for a lot more input as to how the school was run. As we have grown over the years, we just assumed that we knew best. I think what this suggestion really means is that we need to give some weight back to the students. If we take their advice, we would probably operate the school in a way that will retain more people."

The next idea, "Clone your existing students", was a good reminder of the old rule of business; learn all you can about your current customers and find more just like them. When we got to "Invite the island of Malta", it took a while to figure out what it really meant. The best ideas can present the most challenge, with the truth of the idea hidden. This is when it is easy to give up and focus only on the ideas that make sense. If you fall into this trap, you won't develop market-disruptive, ground-breaking products or services; you will just fall back into old tactics like mailing out a new brochure. Later, you will be left wondering why the phones aren't ringing.

When we examined "Invite the island of Malta", we realized that, even though we were located in the ethnically diverse Minneapolis/St. Paul metropolitan area, almost all of our students were Caucasian. We had always wondered why our student population wasn't more diverse. What we taught wasn't geared only toward a Caucasian student. The classes were welcoming to everyone who attended. The *island of Malta* suggestion made us realize that, in a sense, our classes were our company's way of hosting a party. When we marketed our classes, we were inviting guests to join our party. No one comes to a party unless they are invited. We needed to expand our marketing to include everyone we wanted to join the party, not just the narrow market we had been focusing on.

We made some small changes in our business practices and marketing to achieve the goal of doubling the size of our school in twelve months. It didn't cost any more than we were currently spending. We reached our goal in eight months.

Step Six-Categorize

Gary Jader likes to call this step *clumping*. You simply take all the ideas and clump them together in obvious groups. Some ideas will all have something to do with the image of the organization; a marketing focus. Other ideas will focus on specific products or services. Others will relate to client or customer relations. Categorizing allows you to look at all your ideas more clearly.

Often, a company will decide they aren't concerned about branding or image, so the ideas in the Image category will be stored for later consideration. Some companies will take one idea from each category to ensure that their efforts are balanced. Categorizing also allows for easy implementation later on. If you want to maintain forward momentum, you can choose to implement one new idea from each category every year. If an organization devoted effort into that simple process, new energy would be continually pumped throughout the company.

Step Seven – Prioritize & Strategize

This step is another reason you want a smaller number of people involved in the Implementation Phase. Deciding the priorities of the organization is not the job of the rank-and-file. Those folks are great at offering suggestions to help you achieve the goal, but they can't determine priorities for the company. Years ago, a member of our Board of Directors gave me a great example of how leadership and front-line should interact. The front-line employees are like a group of people chopping a path through a jungle. The leaders are a smaller group of people sitting on top of a tall pole. The people on the pole are in charge of looking ahead and occasionally shouting down directions to the group chopping the path. "There is a big boulder ahead, turn left." "A storm is coming, stop chopping and take shelter." The job of the people on the pole is to look ahead to try to help the company avoid future problems, or to make sure the front-line folks are all moving in the same direction.

If the people on the pole ever climbed down and helped chop the path, the path would be chopped faster, but no one would know where they were going. There would be no direction. If the people chopping the path climbed up the pole, everyone would have a wonderful view, but nothing would ever get done. It is good for each side to briefly experience what the other does so they know how to best serve each other, but they should spend their time performing their function for the benefit of the entire organization.

The Prioritize & Strategize step is simple; decide which outcomes are important enough for immediate implementation, which ideas go into *the vault* for later use, and which ideas go bye-bye.

It is a risk that ideas that go into the vault may never again see the light of day. This is a common mistake after organizations finish brainstorming. They focus so tightly on the immediate ideas that they forget about all the cool stuff sitting in a drawer. Put a reminder in your calendar to review the vault once a year.

Strategizing is a big part of the process, but since it involves company-specific decisions, I can offer little advice or information. Just be sure to include the following:

- Who will lead an idea through implementation?
- What resources will be allocated?
- What is the timeline for each stage of implementation?
- How will progress be communicated to others?
- What danger signs will lead to discontinuing a plan?
- Exactly what does a successful outcome look like?

Step Eight-Rewardize

Yes, I made up the word *Rewardize*, but it had to match Categorize, Strategize, and Prioritize.

Typically, the only people rewarded within a company are those who cross the finish line, forgetting all those who helped the individual get there. Frankly, I think it is appalling how much is spent on celebrations for the sales department compared to administrative support or IT. While the sales force is partying on a lake cruise with prime rib and cabernet, the support staff gets bagels in the break room.

Be that as it may, be sure to reward everyone involved in the process, not just those who saw a concept to the end. Those who took their time to brainstorm and develop the list of ideas you needed should get just as big a pat on the back. I am not suggesting a bonus check for everyone in the room. In fact, money has been discovered to be a disincentive for most people. In *Influence*, Dr. Cialdini cites a study where people were asked to take part in a program that could potentially yield great benefits for the safety in their neighborhoods (getting drivers to behave more conscientiously behind the wheel). Because the participants in the study saw themselves as concerned about safety, they were happy to put up yard signs to promote the program. Later, when they were offered money to continue the program beyond its expiration, the number of willing participants decreased.

People act based on how they view themselves; what are their most important values. Offering money removes the connection between the act and the self-image, so commitment decreases. The best rewards are personal, do some digging into each individual and reward them accordingly. I wanted to thank two employees in our company for going above and beyond their duties. At first, I thought of restaurant gift certificates, but that would seem commonplace. Since the two employees worked closely with our Artistic Director, Pamela Mayne, I asked her advice. She said, "Theresa is a girly girl. She loves to pamper herself, so get her a gift certificate to a spa. John, on the other hand, loves video gaming. Get him a gift certificate to a video game store." I followed Pamela's advice, which has never steered me wrong.

When I gave Theresa and John their gift cards, you would have thought by their reaction that I gave them each a new car. Because the gifts had some thought behind them, they meant so much more. Ask around the office about each person and reward them with something that will be remembered, not just redeemed.

Read This Last

This is the part of the book most people skip, so I decided to put some really valuable pieces of advice to rewardize those who stayed committed until the very end.

One bit of advice I recommend is to remember what I wrote at the beginning of this book; the words of the CEO who said, "We want a lot of new and exciting ideas, but we don't really want to change anything." In order for brainstorming to live, something has to die. What dies is often the rigid adherence to old methods; along with ego, fear, and complacency.

Who will champion the idea?

A crucial component to the success of a new initiative is what many call an *Idea Champion*. It is this person's responsibility to see the idea through to completion; often, battling obstacles along the way. Too often, the position of idea champion is simply thrust upon the person who created the idea in the first place. There are two problems with this practice. One is that, in effective idea generation, there should be so much input that you really don't have just one person to thank for the idea. Another reason is that the person selected to champion the idea must not only have the authority to carry the idea over various hurdles; he or she must also have the personality that does not shrink from opposition.

A wonderful example of an idea champion is Muhammad Yunus. Yunus was born in 1940 in Bangladesh, a small country in south Asia. He grew up to be a successful businessman, politician, and scholar; earning a Ph.D. in Economics from Vanderbilt University in the United States. He was always concerned about the level of poverty in Bangladesh. He knew that one of the gravest concerns for the poor was the practice of "loan sharking." In order to survive, poor people would have to borrow money. Since banks would never loan money to a poor person, loan sharks would offer loans with interest rates so high the poor would be in debt to the loan shark forever.

While head of the economics department at Chittagong University in Bangladesh, Yunus began researching poverty reduction. While visiting poverty-stricken homes in the village of Jobra, he discovered that it would take very little money to help families get out of debt and create small businesses through which to sustain themselves. His prime concern was getting people enough money that they would not have to resort to borrowing from loan sharks. So, he took twenty-seven dollars from his own pocket and made the first of what would later be known as a *microloan*. Before you think to yourself, "What could someone accomplish with just twenty-seven dollars?" you should know that the money was divided among forty-two women in the village.

When asked what the interest was on the loan, Yunus replied, "I am not charging any interest, and there is no time limit to repay. I do want you to pay back the loan, but only when you can." Yunus discovered just how resourceful people can be when given the chance. These women created small businesses that brought in money enough to pay back the loan as well as sustain their families. Here is where the idea champion part comes into play. Seeing how simple and affordable his idea was, Yunus went to banks in Bangladesh. He told them about how they could help end poverty in their country, and about how small an investment it would take. The bank executives laughed at him. They told him that it was foolish to give loans to poor people because they were too much of a risk. It had never been done before, they were not going to start now, and he was a dupe to fall for their "begging." Ego, fear, and complacency all rolled into one.

Yunus tried explaining that he had already experimented with one loan and that it was paid back quickly with a small interest. The banks said that it might have worked with a few people, but would never work on a broader scale. So Yunus tried expanding his microloans to the entire village of Jobra. When this proved successful, he went back to the banks. They said it might have worked in

Jobra, but would never be successful outside of the village. Yunus expanded the microloan program to more villages. Each time he was successful, the banks said the microloan program was flawed in its conception and they refused to participate.

He eventually wore the bank executives down; there is only so long a person can deny success when it is put right in front of you. He founded Grameen Bank ("Village Bank") in 1983 based on the concept of *microfinance*. To date, Grameen Bank has loaned billions of dollars, has a ninety-five percent payback rate, and Yunus was awarded the Nobel Peace Prize in 2006. If he had not championed his idea with conviction, if he had listened to the bank "experts," thousands of people would be trapped in a cycle of poverty to this day. Sometimes the only response to, "It can't be done" is "It just hasn't been done yet."

Burn the boats!

When Hernando Cortez landed on the shores of Mexico in 1519 with the intent of seizing the riches of the Aztecs, he and his men were greatly outnumbered by the Aztec warriors. In order to gain absolute commitment, Cortez ordered all their ships to be burned; believing that having no escape would steel his men's resolve. When his men refused, Cortez called out, "We will return in *their* ships." The ships were burned. With the possibility of retreat no longer at hand, the Spaniards conquered the Aztecs.

I do not suggest burning your ships, but be ready to sink a few. Good luck!

References

Brown, S. (2009). *Play*. New York: Penguin Group

Cialdini, R. (2001). *Influence: Science and Practice*. 4th ed. Needham Heights: Allyn and Bacon

Gladwell, M. (2005). *Blink: The Power of Thinking without Thinking*. 1st ed. New York: Little Brown & Company

Graham, J., Sarfati, S., Mason, M., Robertson, S., Skillman, K., Williams, B. (2006). *Seven Measures of Success*. Washington DC: ASAE & The Center for Association Leadership

Haidt, J. (2006). *Happiness Hypothesis, The*. Cambridge: Basic Books

Johnstone, K. (1981). *Impro: Improvisation and the Theatre*. New York: Routledge

Lehrer, J. (2012). *Imagine: How Creativity Works*. New York: Houghton Mifflin Harcourt

Lipkin, N., Perrymore, A. (2009) *Y in the Workplace*. Franklin Lakes: Career Press

Pausch, R. (2008). *The Last Lecture*. New York: Hyperion

Provine, R. (2000). *Laughter: A Scientific Investigation*. New York: Penguin Group

Spolin, V. (1963). *Improvisation for the Theatre*. Evanston: Northwestern University Press

About the Author

Stephen "Stevie Ray" Rentfrow was born a small boy, which worked out so well he decided to remain one. Stevie co-founded *Stevie Ray's Improv Company* in 1989 and continues to run it with his partner, Pamela Mayne. He is a nationally syndicated columnist for the Business Journal Newspapers, a corporate trainer, and keynote speaker.

Stevie Ray is the only person in the country to design his own college degree, *Theory and Performance of Comedy* (his parents were *so* proud). He has he toured the country performing with such stars as "Weird Al" Yankovic, Paula Poundstone, Marsha Warfield of *Night Court,* and Rich Hall of *Saturday Night Live.* He is a lot funnier on stage than he is in this book.

A martial artist since 1977, he has studied seven martial arts and holds four black belts in four of them. At one point in his career he was a bodyguard for Pee Wee Herman (yes, really).

Stevie is also a beekeeper and producer of *Steve's Bees Minnesota Honey* and a volunteer for the Minnesota State Services for the Blind, recording books on tape for the blind.

Stevie lives in Minneapolis with his wife, Kanitta and step-daughter, Ondine.

Other books by Stevie Ray

About the Rent
One Thousand Punches a Day
Quick Thinking for Any Situation
Speaking in Public without Sweating in Private
Spontaneity Takes Practice
The Birth, Life, (and sometimes death),
  of a Comedian
Three Big Words
What We Laugh At... and Why
Working the Room: Networking for Professionals

www.ingramcontent.com/pod-product-compliance
Lightning Source LLC
Chambersburg PA
CBHW052158220526
45471CB00004B/1725